The
AMERICAN
REVOLUTION
and the
POLITICS
of
LIBERTY

The
AMERICAN REVOLUTION
and the
POLITICS
of
LIBERTY

ROBERT H. WEBKING

Louisiana State University Press
Baton Rouge and London

97 96 95 94 93 92 91 90 89 88   5 4 3 2 1

Designer: Laura Roubique Gleason
Typeface: Trump Mediaeval
Typesetter: The Composing Room of Michigan, Inc.
Printer: Thomson-Shore, Inc.
Binder: John H. Dekker & Sons, Inc.

Library of Congress Cataloging-in-Publication Data

Webking, Robert H., 1951—
    The American Revolution and the politics of liberty / Robert H.
Webking.
        p.   cm.
    Includes index.
    ISBN 0-8071-1438-3 (alk. paper)
    1. United States—Politics and government—Revolution, 1776–1783.
2. Political science—United States—History—18th century.
3. Statesmen—United States—History—18th century.   I. Title.
E10.W4 1988   88-11777
973.3—dc19   CIP

Portions of the Introduction and Chapter Eight appeared, in slightly different form,
in Robert Webking and Gary J. Schmitt, "Revolutionaries, Antifederalists, and
Federalists: Comments on Gordon Wood's Understanding of the American
Founding," *Political Science Reviewer*, IX (Fall, 1979), 195–229, and are reprinted by
permission. Another portion of Chapter Eight appeared, in somewhat different form,
in "Virtue and Individual Rights in John Adams' *Defence*," *Interpretation*, XIII
(May, 1985), 177–93, and is reprinted by permission.

To Donna

Contents

Preface   ix

Acknowledgments   xiii

Abbreviations   xv

Introduction   1

ONE • *James Otis*   16

TWO • *Patrick Henry*   30

THREE • *John Dickinson*   41

FOUR • *Samuel Adams*   61

FIVE • *John Adams*   78

SIX • *Thomas Jefferson*   92

SEVEN • *Liberty*   110

EIGHT • *Liberty and Virtue*   125

NINE • *Liberty and Political Prudence*   153

Index   177

Preface

The subject of this book is the political thought of the intellectual leaders of the American Revolution. I seek to clarify the arguments about human beings and their governments made by the most thoughtful and influential of the American revolutionaries to explain their opposition to the policies of the British government during the period immediately preceding the American war for independence.

The Americans explained their resistance to the British in principled terms. They claimed that British actions were not merely unwise or impolitic but fundamentally wrong or unjust. And the Americans did not merely assert the injustice of British actions; they argued it. They defended the position that there are certain fundamental principles according to which just governments must act, and they developed careful and complex arguments to persuade others, in the colonies and in Britain, that the British government was violating those principles to an extent that prudent, well-informed citizens could not allow. This book is about those principles and those arguments.

This work differs in its focus from most works written by students of American political thought about the founding principles of the American regime. Such students tend to concentrate on the thought behind the Constitution and rarely go further with the revolutionaries than to consider Thomas Jefferson and the Declaration of Independence. Most texts on American political thought barely mention the period before 1776. It in no way diminishes the importance of understanding James Madison and Alexander Hamilton, however, to suggest that the arguments of John Dickinson, James Otis, and Samuel Adams also merit serious attention.

In its approach to the political thought of the American revolutionaries, this work differs from works written by historians. As the introduction details, historians in recent decades have come to realize that
the American Revolution cannot be explained without considering
the ideas that led the revolutionaries to act as they did. Yet, despite
their realization, they have not analyzed the political thought of the
period in all of its intricacy.

That historians have not presented a careful and systematic consideration of the political theory behind the Revolution may follow
from the fact that the principal objective of the historical scholar is
not to understand political thought in and of itself. That is to say,
because virtually all major commentaries on the political thought of
the American Revolution are undertaken from a historical point of
view, they approach that thought with the purpose of explaining
something other than the arguments. These studies see the arguments surrounding the American Revolution as interesting because
they help to explain the fact that some colonies of Great Britain on
the North American continent fought a war for independence between 1775 and 1783. My interest in the arguments of the American
Revolution, by contrast, is that of a student of political thought—an
interest in the arguments themselves. My direct concern is not to
note that the Americans believed certain things and that those convictions led them to revolt but to understand the content of the
American arguments. I seek to analyze the thought of the American
revolutionaries in its complexity and thereby to appreciate its assumptions, its internal tensions, and its implications.

I attempt to avoid taking the statements of the revolutionaries out
of the context in which their authors originally placed them. A term,
phrase, sentence, or paragraph from an argument cannot be understood adequately except as a part of the whole argument. Samuel
Adams' forceful denunciations of the British government as tyrannical, for example, can be neither understood nor evaluated without
considering them in the context of his discussions of the meanings of
both tyranny and liberty, and of the reasons why seemingly minor
governmental actions may have very serious implications for making
one or the other more possible. Similarly, Adams' stated desire for
peace and stability may seem disingenuous unless placed in the context of his broader political argument.

The appreciation of complex political thought requires care and
patience from the student. Judgments that particular points are important or unimportant, reasonable or unreasonable, may be made

legitimately only when the complete argument is understood. To lay out these arguments in all their complexity is my aim in this book. In chapters one through six, I examine carefully the arguments about political principles and policies put forward by six major American leaders of the period preceding the Revolution. I analyze each of the six independently from the others in order to demonstrate the argument of each on its own terms. Only after an analysis of each leader do I draw conclusions about the arguments that guided the American revolutionaries in general (chapters seven through nine), for the political thought of the Revolution itself can be adequately understood only when one knows well the political thought of the most important revolutionaries.

Because my major concern is political thought, I do not distract the reader from this subject by presenting extended discussions of political events. Rather, I seek to clarify the Americans' own explanations of their behavior. My study, then, precludes discussing factors other than those expressed in the leading Americans' arguments that might have led some Americans to seek independence, or discussing why the British did what they did during that period. I assume the reader to be familiar with the Boston Tea Party, the Townshend Acts, the Stamp Act, and other important acts and events of the period. My goal is to make the reader more familiar with the intricate arguments made by the revolutionaries at the time of those events—arguments about human beings and politics explaining why they believed their resistance to British actions to be just.

Although my purpose is to explain political thought rather than all of the factors that produced the American Revolution, I submit that one cannot understand why the Revolution happened without a clear comprehension of the political principles embraced by its leaders. The conclusions reached here, therefore, contribute much to an understanding of the historical causes of the Revolution.

Furthermore, this commentary on the thought of the American Revolution has bearing on other political issues. One set of important implications has to do with the meaning of the American regime. The arguments the Americans made in the period preceding the Revolution are about how a government should rule a people. The principles they discussed and refined during that period have formed the foundation of American politics ever since. Thus, an understanding of the political arguments of the Americans before 1776 yields, in addition to an understanding of the political thought of the Revolution, an understanding of the issues, disputes, and tensions surrounding the writing and adoption of the Constitution, as well as an understanding of the issues surrounding the dispute over slavery—to mention only the two most crucial periods when belief in those principles was tested and implemented.

The implications of this study go even further. In the Declaration of Independence the Americans write of their "decent respect for the opinions of mankind" and declare their desire that "facts be submitted to a candid world" to demonstrate the justice of their revolution. This concern with the opinions of rational people regardless of nationality demonstrates a point frequently made by the revolutionaries: they believed that their cause was the cause of mankind and that, therefore, all reasonable people would understand the justice of their actions. They understood their cause to be universal because, they argued, their right to and desire for liberty were things derived not from particular historical circumstances but from human nature. In studying the American arguments about the principles that ought to guide politics and the justice of employing revolution in their name, we can perhaps gain some perspective on other revolutions that have existed, do exist, or will exist in the world. We can use the Americans' arguments to increase our understanding of what human beings sometimes find important enough to fight for and to help us weigh the justice of their revolutionary behavior.

Acknowledgments

This project began when Gary J. Schmitt asked me to work with him on an article about differences between the thought of the American revolutionaries and the thought of the authors of the Constitution. After writing the article, we decided that a more lengthy study of the revolutionaries' arguments was needed, and we began the work. This book is the end product of that work. We designed it together and began writing it together. Gary had written part of what is now the Introduction when it became clear to him that other commitments would make him unable to continue with the project. Much of what is good in this book is due to his input. Any errors in fact or interpretation are mine.

I am grateful to Ryan Barilleaux and Donna Mellen, who read portions of the manuscript and offered useful suggestions. The work benefited from the thoughtful criticisms made by Robert A. Becker and Norman A. Graebner, who read the manuscript for Louisiana State University Press. Finally, I thank my colleagues at the University of Texas at El Paso, especially C. Richard Bath and Z. Anthony Kruszewski, for their constant support and encouragement.

Abbreviations

JO   James Otis, *The Rights of the British Colonists Asserted and Proved*. In *Pamphlets of the American Revolution, 1750–1776*, ed. Bernard Bailyn. Cambridge, Mass., 1965.

JD   Paul Leicester Ford, ed. *The Political Writings of John Dickinson, 1764–1774*. New York, 1970.

PWD   *Political Writings of John Dickinson*. 2 vols. Wilmington, 1801.

SA   Harry Alonzo Cushing, ed. *The Writings of Samuel Adams*. 4 vols. New York, 1904.

JA   Charles Francis Adams, ed. *The Works of John Adams*. 10 vols. Boston, 1850–56.

TJ   Julian P. Boyd, ed. *The Papers of Thomas Jefferson*. 21 vols. Princeton, 1950.

The
AMERICAN
REVOLUTION
and the
POLITICS
of
LIBERTY

Introduction

For much of this century it was the accepted opinion that an examination of the arguments made by the American revolutionaries would yield no important knowledge. Scholarship during the first half of this century was dominated by historians who minimized, if not denigrated, the place of ideas in the genesis of the American Revolution. Known collectively as the Progressives, these historians turned to material interests, class structure, property holdings—in general, to socioeconomic factors—to explain the revolutionaries' behavior. They believed the revolutionaries to have been moved by what was in their pockets, not by what was in their heads; or rather, more generally, they believed that what is in human beings' pockets controls what is in their heads.

The Progressives' work was the culmination of a long process of disparaging the scholarship of such men as George Bancroft and Sir George Otto Trevelyan, the so-called Whig historians. Bancroft's *History of the United States* and Trevelyan's *The American Revolution*, both written in the nineteenth century, depicted the American Revolution as a high point in the emergence of freedom and liberty in the English-speaking world. The tone of these works was lofty, but the history was soft. The Whig historians appeared to be partisans of the process they were describing, so they were easy targets for the historians of the early twentieth century trained in the new, objective methods of "scientific" history.

The first effective assault upon the American revolutionaries' commitment to their professed ideals came with the publication of George Louis Beer's *British Colonial Policy, 1754–1765* in 1907 and Charles McLean Andrews' *Colonial Background of the American*

1

Revolution in 1924. Both works seriously questioned the sincerity of the principled claims the Americans made. Their primary piece of evidence was the fact that in the decade and a half leading up to 1776, the colonists' arguments tended to shift every time the British put forward a new policy that met the Americans' principled objections to the previous policy. If there was an American commitment, this evidence seemed to say, it had little to do with principle and must, therefore, have had to do with economic expediency.

For Andrews it was no surprise to find that the Americans were not controlled by their stated principles. He believed that events move men and not the reverse, and thus that revolutions are brought about not by human intent but by forces beyond human control. As he stated in his presidential address before the American Historical Association in 1925, historical circumstances are the "masters, not the servants, of statesmen and political agitators."[1] In effect, Andrews was indicating that historians do not have to address the question of whether the arguments made by the Americans were reasonable, for the arguments were of no importance in bringing about the Revolution. What needed to be understood, he insisted, were not the arguments but the impersonal forces that dictated to the colonists that they argue.

The identity of those impersonal forces had been suggested a few years before Andrews' address in Charles Beard's *An Economic Interpretation of the Constitution*, published in 1913. Beard claimed that economic forces were the cause both of great movements in politics and, in particular, of the Constitution's being written as it was. All that needed to be done to explain the American Revolution was to apply Beard's insight about events in 1787 to the events leading up to 1776.

The most important works to apply economic determinism to the Revolution were Charles H. Lincoln's *The Revolutionary Movement in Pennsylvania, 1760-1776*, Carl Becker's *History of Political Parties in the Province of New York, 1760-1776*, and Arthur Meier Schlesinger's *The Colonial Merchants and the American Revolution*, appearing in 1901, 1909, and 1918, respectively. The general thrust of these and other works that followed was made clear by Schlesinger in an article he published soon after his book had appeared. There he states that the Revolution cannot be properly under-

---

1. Charles McLean Andrews, "The American Revolution: An Interpretation," *American Historical Review*, XXXI (1926), 219ff.

stood if examined as though it were a "great forensic controversy over abstract governmental rights." Rather, the Revolution is only comprehensible when "the clashing of economic interests and the interplay of mutual prejudices, opposing ideals and personal antagonisms" has been fully explored.[2]

What is perhaps most striking in the Progressive interpretation of the revolutionary period is the degree to which the struggle between the colonies and England is subsumed by the internal struggles within the various colonies. That is, for these historians the real war was fought not between buckskin-clad youths and red-coated veterans but between the classes then existing in each of the colonies. The constitutional debate that arose, therefore, was a debate between various domestic interest groups, each using the language of political principle to defend its economic position.

According to the Progressives, the arguments of the revolutionaries were mere propaganda designed to achieve support for the actions they desired, their reasons having little to do with their arguments but more to do with desires for power and money. Attempts to prove this contention can be found in John Chester Miller's *Sam Adams: Pioneer in Propaganda*, published in 1936, and in Philip Davidson's *Propaganda and the American Revolution*, published in 1941. Both works argue that leaders of the Revolution were demagogues whose behavior was best explained not by what they were saying but by where their narrow, selfish advantage lay. Davidson, for example, claims that the arguments put forward by the likes of John Hancock and Samuel Adams were nothing more than "the propagandist's rationalization of his desire to protect his vested interests."[3]

Even works such as Carl Becker's 1922 study, *The Declaration of Independence: A Study in the History of Political Ideas*, which was ostensibly concerned with the ideas of the revolutionary period, views the arguments of the revolutionaries as merely rhetorical strategies, as ideas neither interesting in themselves nor useful for explaining the Americans' behavior. Becker assumes that historians ought to be concerned with these ideas only to the degree that they were—like the Continental Army, for example—weapons to be wielded in the struggle with London. Indeed, according to Becker's understanding, the ideas of the colonists were like the army in an-

2. Arthur Meier Schlesinger, "The American Revolution Reconsidered," *Political Science Quarterly*, XXXIV (March, 1919), 61ff.

3. Philip Davidson, *Propaganda and the American Revolution* (Chapel Hill, 1941), 46.

other way: they could be changed around and moved from place to place as events required. Becker argues that the colonists were not intellectually consistent throughout the revolutionary period but rather changed their arguments as circumstances changed in order to pursue their vested interests more effectively. "Thus step by step, from 1764 to 1776, the colonists modified their theory to suit their needs."[4] It was not political theory that was important to the colonists, then, and consequently that theory cannot explain their actions during the revolutionary period. What was important was real selfish needs.

By World War II the cynicism engendered by the Progressive interpretation of the American Revolution had begun to wane. In the context of the politics of Stalin and of Hitler, the principles enunciated by the founders began to take on a new life. Becker, for instance, in the preface to his 1942 edition of *The Declaration*, suggests that events "have forced men everywhere to re-appraise the validity of half-forgotten ideas" expressed by Jefferson and his colleagues.[5] By the following year Becker was less tentative: "In respect to fundamentals, Jefferson's political philosophy is still valid for us. . . . [We accept the republican form of government] for the same fundamental reason that Jefferson accepted it—from the profound conviction that it is the only form of government that is not at war with the natural rights of mankind."[6] The thought seemed to be that because men were moved to defend a political system that sought to secure their natural rights in 1941, it was possible that those same principles might have moved men once before. History would appear to have taught the historians a lesson.

Much of the work of the next generation of historians was taken up with dismantling the scholarly edifice erected by the Progressives. The most important first step in this process of resurrecting the integrity of the revolutionaries was taken by Edmund S. Morgan and Helen M. Morgan in their 1953 study, *The Stamp Act Crisis: Prologue to Revolution*. In opposition to the Progressives, they argued that the colonial position regarding Parliament's power to tax the Americans was from the first quite consistent. By 1765 the Americans had clearly articulated the position that they continued to hold until they

4. Carl L. Becker, *The Declaration of Independence: A Study in the History of Political Ideas* (New York, 1922), 133.

5. *Ibid.*, viii.

6. Carl L. Becker, "What Is Still Living in the Political Philosophy of Thomas Jefferson?" in Philip Snyder (ed.), *Detachment and the Writing of History: Essays and Letters of Carl L. Becker* (Ithaca, 1958), 232, 238.

cut all ties with England in 1776: Parliament had no authority to tax the colonies, regardless of whether the taxes were "internal" or "external," if their main purpose was to raise revenue. On the other hand, argued the Morgans, the Americans rather consistently accepted the prerogative of Parliament to enact legislation affecting them when the legislation concerned regulating the affairs of the empire. By demonstrating the consistency of the American position, the Morgans' analysis put to rest the Progressives' portrayal of colonists as chameleonlike people who changed the complexion of their arguments to suit changes in events.

The second major step in overturning the Progressive interpretation of the American Revolution was to attack their depiction of the domestic colonial scene. In the 1950s and early 1960s, a series of studies critically reviewed the picture of colonial America as riddled with internal economic and class conflict. Works such as Robert E. Brown and B. Katherine Brown's *Middle-Class Democracy and the Revolution in Massachusetts, 1691-1780* in 1955 and their *Virginia, 1705-1786: Democracy or Aristocracy?* in 1964 showed the class stratification that the Progressive interpretation had assumed existed in the colonies to be of little strength. And according to Jackson Turner Main in his 1965 study, *The Social Structure of Revolutionary America*, even where some broad class structures did exist, the lack of poverty and the presence of general social mobility kept tensions between members of different classes at a minimum. In general, the literature of the 1950s and 1960s concluded that material differences within the American colonies could not have been the decisive factor in causing the revolutionaries' behavior. The evidence instead proved that the Progressive historians' understanding of the things that led the Americans to act as they did was faulty.

The realization that the Progressives' understanding of the American Revolution is inadequate has led historians to return to the Americans' own explanations of their behavior in order to account for the Revolution. Most important among these recent historians is Bernard Bailyn, who has presented his account of the Revolution in three books: *The Ideological Origins of the American Revolution*, *The Origins of American Politics*, and *The Ordeal of Thomas Hutchinson*. Bailyn claims that his interpretation is superior to those of the Whig and Progressive historians because it is based upon "an inclusiveness of sympathy and a degree of comprehensiveness in data that distinguish this interpretation from its predecessors."[7]

7. Bernard Bailyn, *The Ordeal of Thomas Hutchinson* (Cambridge, 1974), ix.

Bailyn begins *Ideological Origins* by quoting from a letter from John Adams to Thomas Jefferson: "What do we mean by the Revolution? The war? That was no part of the Revolution; it was only an effect and consequence of it. The Revolution was in the minds of the people." According to Bailyn it is this revolution in ideas that one must understand first. In order to comprehend the actions taken by the colonists, one must look to men's thoughts. "We shall not understand why there was a revolution until we suspend disbelief and listen with care to what the Revolutionaries themselves said was the reason there was a revolution." Bailyn thus rejects the Progressive view that the ideas expressed by the Americans were, at best, clever rhetoric, and argues instead that the colonists were sincere in their arguments. He reminds his readers that "the eighteenth century was an age of ideology; the beliefs and fears expressed on one side of the Revolutionary controversy were as sincere as those expressed on the other."[8]

Bailyn's specific argument is that the colonial American mind, along with the Revolution it produced, was a product of seventeenth- and eighteenth-century British opposition thought. He writes that the American mind was formed by a variety of sources: classical thought, the Enlightenment, common law, and Puritan theology. But "what brought these disparate strands of thought together . . . and shaped it into a coherent whole, was the influence of still another group of writers," the radical Whigs. These opposition theorists and publicists, "more than any other single group of writers . . . shaped the mind of the American Revolutionary generation." Bailyn thus places the ideological origins of the American Revolution in the writings of England's radical Whigs. What in England was an intellectual movement of only minor importance became in America, by a process "so swift . . . as to seem almost instantaneous," the dominant mode of thought.[9]

For Bailyn, what distinguishes the mainstream of British thinkers from these dissenters was that those in the mainstream "spoke mainly with pride of the constitutional and political achievements of Georgian England." The dissenters looked at Britain "with alarm, stressed the dangers to England's ancient heritage and the loss of pristine virtue, studied the processes of decay, and dwelt endlessly on the evidence of corruption they saw about them and the dark future

8. Bernard Bailyn, *The Ideological Origins of the American Revolution* (Cambridge, 1967), 1, 158; Bailyn, *The Origins of American Politics* (New York, 1968), 11.
9. Bailyn, *Ideological Origins*, 34–35.

these malignant signs portended." Adherents of the dissenting tradition in both England and America were always anticipating an attack, always expecting to find a "conspiracy" against the liberties they were constantly struggling to uphold. It was this opposition view of politics, and especially the dominating fear of conspiracy against liberty, writes Bailyn, that was "determinative of the political understanding of eighteenth-century Americans."[10]

Bailyn argues that the Americans were sincere in the beliefs they held as a heritage from the English dissenters. Sincerity, however, is not the test of rationality. Bailyn tells us that the American Revolution had its origin in ideology, but he never pauses to define the term. One meaning that *ideology* has come to assume is simply political principles. A more precise meaning of *ideology* is a simplistic set of convictions that distorts perception of political reality and clouds the distinction between the politically desirable and the politically possible. Ideology in this second meaning is the opposite of political prudence. Political ideologues are so blinded by their convictions that they cannot act as prudent statesmen do: on the basis of understanding the needs and aspirations of their fellow citizens as well as understanding the ability of political action to meet those needs and aspirations. Insofar as Bailyn is unclear as to what he means by the ideology of the Americans, he has left unanswered a serious question about the causes, and rationality, of the American Revolution. There is, however, much evidence in his work to suggest that he has answered the question. And the evidence suggests that Bailyn's contention is precisely this: the revolutionary Americans were acting in irrational ways because they were determined to do so by an ideological paranoia that gripped them and left them incapable both of perceiving political reality and of acting politically like rational human beings.

That Bailyn understands the difference between the reasonable and the ideological is clear in the following passage: "American resistance in the 1760s and 1770s was a response to acts of power deemed arbitrary, degrading, and uncontrollable—a response, in itself objectively reasonable, that was inflamed to the point of explosion by ideological currents generating fears everywhere in America." The ideology, then, led the Americans to act not as rational, prudent statesmen but as irrational ideologues moved by "inflamed sensibilities—exaggerated distrust and fear."[11]

10. Bailyn, *American Politics*, 46, 56.

11. Bernard Bailyn, "The Central Themes of the American Revolution, an Interpretation," in Stephen G. Kurtz and James H. Hutson (eds.), *Essays on the American Revolution* (Chapel Hill, 1973), 13.

According to Bailyn, the Americans, by adopting the thought of the opposition party, saw conspiracies against their liberties where none in fact existed. By this argument, it was not so much the assertion of British authority in their lives as the colonists' interpretation of that assertion that led them into rebellion. Through a thorough assimilation of the writings of the radical Whigs, the colonists had developed a habit of mind that precluded a reasonable assessment of the situation. They were controlled by "beliefs and passions that grip[ped] people's minds."[12] In short, the Americans' convictions not only led to their reactions to British political actions but also determined the Americans to see dangers where there were none. As one commentator has summarized Bailyn's position, "the American revolutionaries became in a way as much the victims of their propaganda as was the British government."[13]

The British in general and Governor Thomas Hutchinson of Massachusetts in particular, in Bailyn's view, were unable to stem the revolutionary tide because prudence and reason are virtually helpless in the face of passionately held ideology. In *The Ordeal of Thomas Hutchinson*, Bailyn argues that Hutchinson was a prudent, well-informed, and competent politician who was simply defeated by the "furies." Like the revolutionaries, Hutchinson opposed the Stamp Act and favored liberty. Unlike them, he understood that governmental order and stability required limits to the liberty that could be allowed. To Hutchinson, who knew that although the British had made some mistakes, "No one, in England or America, was plotting to rob the colonists of their freedom," the crisis was artificial. His frequent efforts to quiet the crisis by explaining patiently and rationally in speeches and pamphlets that the colonists' fears were unfounded failed, Bailyn tells us, because the leaders of the Revolution "were not striving to act reasonably or logically." Bailyn concludes *The Ordeal* by writing, "There is no better testimony to the character of the forces that were shaping the revolutionary movement . . . than the failure of so prudent, experienced, and intelligent a man as Thomas Hutchinson to control them." That failure, Bailyn contends, was caused by "the incapacity of sheer logic, of reason, compelling in its own terms but operating within the limits of the received tradition, to control or even fully to comprehend an upsurge of ideological passion."[14]

12. Bailyn, *Ordeal*, vii.
13. Harvey C. Mansfield, Jr., *The Spirit of Liberalism* (Cambridge, 1978), 77–78.
14. Bailyn, *Ordeal*, 97, 380, 75.

Historian Gordon Wood praises Bailyn's work as the first comprehensive view of the Revolution to come to grips with the "fear and frenzy," the "exaggerations," that characterized the ideas of the Americans. Because the Americans were filled with "fanatical and millennial thinking," their actions were "not the product of rational and conscious calculation, but of dimly perceived and rapidly changing thoughts and situations." Under circumstances like those Bailyn describes as existing in the years leading to the American Revolution, writes Wood, "men become more the victim than the manipulators of their ideas." He concludes from Bailyn that "the ideas of the Americans seem, in fact, to form what can only be called a revolutionary syndrome."[15]

Wood analyzes Bailyn's thesis a step further: "By seeking to uncover the motives of the Americans expressed in the Revolutionary pamphlets, Bailyn has ended by demonstrating the autonomy of ideas as phenomena, where the ideas operate, as it were, over the heads of the participants, taking them in directions no one could have foreseen. His discussion of Revolutionary thought thus represents a move back to a deterministic approach to the Revolution."[16] Hence, in spite of the great distance between the Progressives' and Bailyn's interpretations of the American Revolution, there is a core agreement that whatever the colonists were saying and writing, the reality of the situation was something quite different.

Wood writes that Bailyn's argument about the causes of the American Revolution has contributed impetus to a new trend in historiography that has historians attempting to explain the Revolution in psychological terms. The question Bailyn seems to have raised is this: why did the Americans hold to the irrational ideology that led them to revolt? According to Wood: "No one can now deny the prevalence of conspiratory fears among the Revolutionaries. Indeed, historians largely take such fears for granted, and have become preoccupied with explaining why the Revolutionaries should have them. This need to make sense of conspiratorial beliefs seems, more than anything else, to lie behind the extraordinary use of psychology in recent writings about the Revolution. While recognizing that there may be rational explanations for fears of conspiracy, most historians cannot help assuming that such fears are mainly rooted in non-

15. Gordon S. Wood, "Rhetoric and Reality in the American Revolution," in Robert F. Berkhofer, Jr. (ed.), *The American Revolution: The Critical Issues* (Boston, 1971), 121–23.
16. *Ibid.*, 121–22.

rational sources."[17] While he agrees with Bailyn that the "revolution-ary syndrome" is not to be explained by looking to the psychological problems of the individual actors of the revolutionary period, Wood does see that such investigations seem a clear result of Bailyn's view that the Revolution was determined by ideas in the revolutionaries' minds over which they had little or no control.

What Bailyn understands as the cause of the revolutionaries' actions differs from the account they gave of themselves in the most famous document of the revolutionary era, the Declaration of Independence. There Jefferson, expressing, as he later said, "the American mind"—the mind that Bailyn has set out to recover—wrote this:

> Prudence, indeed, will dictate that Governments long established should not be changed for light and transient causes; and accordingly all experience hath shown that mankind are more disposed to suffer, while evils are sufferable, than to right themselves by abolishing the forms to which they are accustomed. But when a long train of abuses and usurpations, pursuing invariably the same Object evinces a design to reduce them under absolute Despotism, it is their right, it is their duty, to throw off such Government, and to provide new Guards for their future security.

The passage speaks of a "design to reduce them under absolute Despotism" and hence might seem to lend credence to Bailyn's argument that the revolutionaries were moved by a tendency to find conspiracy too quickly behind every action of the British government. Reflection on the passage as a whole, however, suggests the opposite. It suggests the belief that people are and should be very slow indeed to reach a conclusion that a despotic design is present. Jefferson and his colleagues display a clear understanding that there are limits to what can be achieved politically. Prudent men, they declare, will not be at all quick to revolt at any evil, for they will realize both the limits of politics and the dangers of revolution. Indeed, the point at which revolution is the course recommended by prudent calculation is an extreme one. Although it is self-evident that human beings have a right to liberty, most of the time that right is best secured by suffer-ing governmental violations to exist. Not only must violations of liberty be neither light nor transient to make revolution prudent, but they must be of the most severe and persistent sort, demonstrating that the government's object is nothing less than absolute despotism.

17. Gordon S. Wood, "Conspiracy and the Paranoid Style: Causality and Deceit in the Eighteenth Century," *William and Mary Quarterly*, XXXIX (1982), 403.

The Americans of this passage, then, speak the language of cautious, prudent, reasonable, and responsible statesmen. They do not speak the simplistic language of ideologues.

Of course it would be possible for men driven by ideology to attempt to appear rational and prudent by using language they didn't mean or by uttering prescriptions they never genuinely followed. Still, the Declaration does suggest that the leaders of the Revolution were moved more by rational calculation and less by irrational ideology than Bailyn concludes. To determine the relative importance of prudence and ideology for the revolutionaries is not an easy task. It requires, as Bailyn recognizes, a careful and comprehensive examination of the revolutionary leaders' explanations of their actions. That examination alone, however, is insufficient, for in order to answer the present question one must be able to make a judgment about seemingly contradictory pieces of evidence. (For example, which is a better indicator of the causes of revolutionary action: the Declaration or the opinions of Thomas Hutchinson?) The best that one can do is to try to enter the thoughts of the revolutionary leaders through the medium of their writings and attempt to appreciate whether they were, as Hutchinson and Bailyn argue, determined to see conspiracy and find some excuse for revolt or, as the Declaration suggests, prudently seeking the most effective available security for their liberties.

Gordon Wood is the second major figure to write of the importance of understanding the ideas of the founding Americans in order for one to understand the American founding. In the preface to his book, *The Creation of the American Republic, 1776-1787,* Wood explains that he began with the intention of writing a monograph on constitution making in the revolutionary period, but found that in order to understand the constitutions it was necessary to understand the political assumptions of the constitution makers. "I needed, in other words, to steep myself in the political literature of the period to the point where the often unspoken premises of thought became clear and explicit."[18]

Wood's monograph became a book of more than six hundred pages. Broader in scope than Bailyn's study, Wood's volume ranges from the Revolution through the writing of the Constitution. His study of the political literature of this era leads him to argue that there was a "fundamental transformation of political culture" in America be-

18. Gordon S. Wood, *The Creation of the American Republic, 1776–1787* (Chapel Hill, 1969), vii–viii.

tween 1776 and 1787. This conclusion is based in part upon a conclusion about the way the Americans as revolutionaries viewed politics. Wood argues that at the time of the Revolution the Americans were moved, not by a modern natural rights conception of the goals of politics, but instead by a view of those goals derived from the political thought of classical antiquity.

In a section entitled "The Ideology of Revolution," Wood attempts to explain the ideological disposition that led the American colonists to revolt. His theme is that "the sacrifice of individual interests to the greater good of the whole formed the essence of republicanism and comprehended for Americans the idealistic goal of the Revolution." Wood is clear in what he means by the greater good of the whole: "This common interest was not, as we might today think of it, simply the sum or consensus of the particular interests that made up the community. It was rather an entity in itself, prior to and distinct from the various private interests of groups and individuals." It is important to note Wood's contention that the public good was "prior to" individual interests. In modern thought individual interests are prior to and form the government. Here the argument is that the common good has priority, or that the purpose of government forms individuals. Indeed, Wood's argument is precisely that the Americans of the Revolution were not moved by a modern understanding of politics, that instead their notion of republicanism "embodied the ideal of the good society as it had been set forth from antiquity through the eighteenth century."[19]

Like Bailyn's argument about the importance of ideology in driving the Americans to revolt, Wood's argument about the content of that ideology is opposed by the language of the Declaration of Independence. The Declaration speaks of unalienable rights—rights that by definition cannot be given up in the name of some transcendent public good or in the name of anything else. Governments are to be judged legitimate or illegitimate according to whether they secure individuals' rights to life, liberty, and the pursuit of happiness, for it is precisely "to secure these rights" that "governments are instituted among men." According to this argument, sacrificing the exercise of some rights will yield a more secure enjoyment of individual rights in the long term. This line of reasoning implies that the public good is the protection of individual liberties against invasion by any individ-

19. *Ibid.*, 53, 58, 59.

ual or group. Legitimate government is to provide the conditions necessary for individuals to pursue their own interests. It seeks a common good that is inseparable from particular interests, not one that is apart from and higher than those interests. By the standard of the Declaration, both the monarchy of George III and Wood's republicanism, in which the public good is prior to individual interests, would be judged to be illegitimate political forms.

Reading Wood, one cannot fail to be impressed by the sheer volume of sources he quotes. Any given paragraph might contain citations to five or ten distinct sources. The book is encyclopedic. The same is true, perhaps to a lesser degree, of Bailyn's works. *Ideological Origins*, for example, is organized topically, with discussions of liberty, power, or conspiracy peppered with quotations of many varied sources to support Bailyn's argument about colonial beliefs.

There are two dangers involved in an analysis of the revolutionaries' thought that is based upon such a liberal use of varied sources at every point. The first danger is that conclusions will be distorted by a failure to take into account the greater importance of some people in bringing about the Revolution. Although both Wood and Bailyn cite some authors and speakers more than others, neither tends to treat the thought of the leaders of the Revolution as more important or more indicative of the thought of the period than that of more obscure people. The second danger is that conclusions might be distorted by the failure to engage in careful, systematic analyses of specific political arguments. Both authors quote phrases or sentences from one source and then move on to another without attempting to place the phrases in the larger context of the work from which they come. Their neglect of context can make it impossible to understand the revolutionary authors' meaning with precision, and indeed can make it seem as if they are arguing something they are not.

I have pointed out that both Bailyn's and Wood's conclusions are opposed by the Declaration of Independence, an important indicator that both analyses of the causes of the American Revolution may be flawed by the problems discussed above. Because they know that to understand the Revolution one must look to the Americans' own explanations of their actions, both authors attempt to explain the ideas behind the Revolution, yet neither presents a sustained discussion of the Declaration, the Americans' most important statement of their position. The neglect of the Declaration is all the more surprising because this important document conflicts with the conclusions

offered by both Wood and Bailyn. One would expect at least a recognition of the problem and some attempt to deal with it from these
historians.

The problems arising from the method followed by Bailyn and
Wood suggest the need to check their findings through a different
method of interpretation. An accurate understanding of the political
thought of the American Revolution requires careful analysis of the
major speeches and writings of the revolutionary leaders, for these are
the works that both formed and stated American opinion. Without
such analysis it is not possible to be confident that one has understood what the revolutionaries meant when they spoke of virtue,
liberty, or tyranny.

Bailyn and Wood have suggested the value of this analysis by turning our attention to the ideas behind the American Revolution, to the
most fruitful source of understanding about the origins of the American regime. They have told us that we cannot understand the American Revolution without understanding that the Americans were
moved to act as they did by the ideas they held. My purpose in undertaking this examination is to attempt to answer the political questions raised by their historical discussions, and my perspective is that
of a student of political thought seeking clarification on the nature
and meaning of those revolutionary ideas.

Some thinkers and writers are vastly more influential than others.
It is possible to identify these leaders whose writings, speeches, and
actions were of prime importance for the Americans during the revolutionary period. They include James Otis, the first great patriot leader in Massachusetts; Patrick Henry, the author of the Virginia Resolves; John Dickinson, the author of the *Farmer's Letters*; Samuel
Adams, Otis' successor as the leader of Massachusetts' patriots; John
Adams, author of the "Novanglus" letters and leader at the Continental Congress; and Thomas Jefferson, the author of the Declaration of
Independence.[20] These leaders, recognized both then and now as the
major figures in American revolutionary thought, did much more
than merely voice the opinions held by the colonists that led them to
revolt; they played a crucial role in shaping those opinions as well, in
teaching the Americans what they ought to do to ensure the health of
their political community. We turn to their thought because it is

20. Bailyn lists the major revolutionary leaders as the two Adamses, Dickinson,
and Jefferson (*American Politics*, 12).

from them that we can elicit most fully and accurately the principles that lie behind the American Revolution.

In order to avoid the danger that immersion in the literature of the revolutionary period might leave the impression that the literature is less argument than a constant repetition of key words, phrases, and slogans, I have chosen to examine the arguments of each of these major figures as a separate whole. Furthermore, where appropriate, I have explored the thought of each leader by concentrating on particular works of special importance. Thus the discussion of James Otis centers on an interpretation of his *Rights of the British Colonies*; the discussion of John Dickinson on the *Farmer's Letters*; the discussion of John Adams on the "Novanglus" letters; and the discussion of Thomas Jefferson on his *Summary View* and on the Declaration of Independence. In each case, I consult other writings from time to time in order to clarify or exemplify particular points, but not enough to distract from the understanding to be gained from the careful, thorough analysis of the complete argument of a key work. The chapters on Patrick Henry and Samuel Adams are different in form. In Henry's case the interpretation is not of a published argument but of a set of resolutions that were of critical importance in moving the colonists to resist the Stamp Act. Samuel Adams wrote extensively throughout the revolutionary period, but no single work of his has the extraordinary importance or thoroughness of the works considered in the other chapters. For that reason, the discussion of Samuel Adams' political thought makes use of a wide selection of writings. Following the examination of these influential leaders, I consider the major arguments that they have in common in order to attempt a judgment on the adequacy of Bailyn's and Wood's general explanations of the political thought of the American Revolution.

ONE

James Otis

The first great intellectual leader of the Americans during the period preceding the Revolution was James Otis of Massachusetts. This fact was noted by John Adams when he wrote, in 1818, "I sincerely believe Mr. Otis to have been the earliest and the principal founder of one of the greatest political revolutions that ever occurred among men."[1] Otis' leadership came through his roles as lawyer, politician, and author. Even before the Stamp Act—the act that first caused widespread concern over the legitimacy of the British government's action on the colonies—had been passed, Otis' understanding of the law led him to object to actions of the British government on the basis that they violated colonial rights.

Otis' first contribution to the American understanding of the relationships among the colonists, their rights, and the British government came in 1761. In the previous year, customs officials in Boston applied to the superior court of the province for writs of assistance, general search warrants that would allow those officials to search wherever and whomever they chose in order more effectively to enforce laws against smuggling. To Otis, and to the merchants who persuaded him to represent them in court against the writs (a task he performed without fee), the writs seemed to pose a grave danger to the rights of individuals.

According to a biographer's account of Otis' long argument against the writs, the Massachusetts lawyer contended that such general warrants were illegal under the British constitution because the unrestricted power to search people "is a power, that places the liberty of

1. *JA*, X, 317.

every man in the hands of every petty officer."[2] The argument, as John Adams recollected it fifty-seven years later, moved from a consideration of the rights of man in a state of nature to a consideration of the contracts men use to form civil society, then to an argument that the natural rights of human beings must be respected by government according to the British constitution, and finally to an argument that the various trade acts the writs were requested to enforce were invalid because they violated the natural and constitutional rights of the colonists.[3]

Whatever the exact content of Otis' speech, clearly it encouraged his fellow colonists to be aware of their rights and to be concerned about governmental violations of those rights. The strength of Otis' appeal led John Adams, in a July 3, 1776, letter to his wife, to date the beginning of the revolutionary crisis at 1761 rather than at 1765 with the Stamp Act. Adams' opinion was always what it was in 1818: "I do say in the most solemn manner, that Mr. Otis' oration against *writs of assistance* breathed into this nation the breath of life." From that time until about 1765 Otis was the leading spokesman for the colonists against the British government.[4]

Otis' credentials were first established in the writs of assistance case, but that was by no means the only thing that made him an important intellectual leader. There was, in addition, his work as politician leading the radicals in the Massachusetts legislature in the first half of the 1760s, and there was also his writing. It is through examining the latter that we can appreciate his argument against the British government and, with it, the argument that shaped American resistance in the early years of the revolutionary crisis.

In 1764 Otis wrote *The Rights of the British Colonies Asserted and Proved*, his most comprehensive work on the subject. This important pamphlet, reprinted in both America and England, was essential reading for "all who kept abreast of affairs on both sides of the Atlantic." It made Otis the most important voice of the American cause. The work was written in the context of parliamentary passage of the Sugar Act and the announcement by George Grenville, Chancellor of the Exchequer, that in the following year he would seek to levy a stamp tax on the colonies. The Sugar Act, passed by Parliament in 1764, laid a tax on molasses imported into the colonies. The tax was actually

---

2. William Tudor, *The Life of James Otis of Massachusetts* (Boston, 1823), 66.
3. *JA*, X, 314–17.
4. *JA*, III, 490, X, 276; see Tudor, *James Otis*, 180, and Bernard Bailyn (ed.), *Pamphlets of the American Revolution, 1750–1776* (Cambridge, 1965), 546, 551.

smaller than the previous duty on molasses, but the higher tax had not in fact been collected (usually because it was less expensive for American traders to bribe customs officials than to pay the tax). The new tax was smaller so that it would be reasonable enough to collect, and its collection would contribute badly needed funds to the British treasury. The Sugar Act was the first in a series of acts passed by Parliament between 1764 and the Revolution with the purpose of taxing the colonies in order to increase British revenues. It thus represents a new departure as, "for the first time in colonial history," Parliament was levying duties not with the purpose of regulating trade (which had been the objective of the previous duties on molasses) but with the purpose of gaining additional revenue from the Americans.5

Otis' argument is that the Sugar Act is a violation of the colonists' constitutional and natural rights, a conclusion he reaches through a discussion of those rights and their bases. Like the speech on the writs of assistance (according to Adams' account), this work bases its conclusion on fundamental grounds. It argues from the purpose and origin of government to the purpose and origin of British government to the justice of a particular sort of action by that government.

Otis begins by noting that there are four different opinions about the origin of government. Some claim that government owes its beginning to the grace of God; others claim it originates in force; still others argue that it begins with contract; and finally some hold that it is founded on property. Regarding the claim that government originates from grace, Otis writes that "mankind seem at this day to be in great measure cured of their madness in this particular, and the notion is pretty generally exploded and hissed off the stage." To say that government is based simply on power or force is unacceptable since it leaves no room for right and wrong and makes the safety of the individual depend upon force alone. As to property, its security is certainly an end of government, but since there are other ends as well, "it will never follow . . . that government is *rightfully* founded on *property* alone."6

Otis finds that many objections are made to the claim that government is founded by contract. He lists objections to the idea of an original contract, to the idea of tacit consent, and to the claim that the

5. Bailyn (ed.), *Pamphlets*, 409, 546; Merrill Jensen, "Commentary," in Randolph G. Adams, *Political Ideas of the American Revolution* (3rd ed.; New York, 1958), 8–9.
6. *JO*, 419, 423.

British government was created by contract at the time of the Glorious Revolution. He concludes this barrage of objections to the contract theory with this: "And, say the opposers of the original compact and of the natural equality and liberty of mankind, will not those answers [to the objections] infallibly show that the doctrine is a piece of *metaphysical* jargon and *systematical* nonsense?" Otis gives a simple answer: "Perhaps not." While he notes the contentions made against the contract theory, Otis does not provide careful answers to those contentions. He seems to take it for granted that his readers will accept the theory as truth without a careful explanation. Otis does, however, offer references for those who might still be in doubt: "I hope the reader will consider that I am at present only mentioning such questions as have been put by highfliers and others in church and state who would exclude all compact between a sovereign and his people, without offering my own sentiments upon them; this however I presume I may be allowed hereafter to do without offense. Those who want a full answer to them may consult Mr. Locke's discourses on government, M. De Vattel's law of nature and nations, and their own consciences."[7]

In a sense, argues Otis, it is correct to say that government owes its being not to contract but to God. God, as the author of nature, has created human beings in such a way that they need society and government in order to get the things they need. What they need—what is the purpose of government—"is above all things to provide for the security, the quiet, and happy enjoyment of life, liberty, and property." If people could ensure these things without government, Otis continues, government would not be needed. Thus, "government is founded *immediately* on the necessities of human nature and *ultimately* on the will of God, the author of nature, who has not left it to men in general to choose whether they will be members of society or not, but at the hazard of their senses if not of their lives."[8] For this reason, it is not simply a matter of human choice that human beings live in society under government. Their nature leads them to do so.

That human beings live under this or that particular government, however, is a fact resulting from choice and contract. Each person, Otis writes, makes a choice at the age of consent as to which society, if any, he will join. A society is made up of equal individuals, each of whom has chosen to become a member. It is up to those individuals

7. *JO*, 422, 420–21.
8. *JO*, 425.

to decide how their society will be governed. "The form of government is by *nature* and by *right* so far left to the *individuals* of each society that they may alter it from a simple democracy or government of all over all to any other form they please. Such alteration may and ought to be made by express compact."⁹

By this point in the pamphlet it has become clear that Otis' argument about the origin of government is not intended to be descriptive. His concern is to discover not how various governments have in fact come to be established but how the just ones must come to be established. As he goes on to note, "for once that it [the establishment of government] has been fairly settled by compact, *fraud, force,* or *accident* have determined it an hundred times." The fact that governments have been established and operated through force, however, does not mean that this process is according to nature, that it is right, that this should happen. Because God, through his authorship of the law of nature, "has given to all men a natural right to be *free*," even "if every prince since *Nimrod* had been a tyrant, it would not prove a *right* to tyrannize."¹⁰

Otis' discussion of the origin of government is one of the most systematic attempts by American politicians and thinkers of the period preceding the Revolution to explain the fundamental philosophical grounds on which their disputes with the government in London were based. It makes sense that Otis would be more concerned with establishing the fundamentals of political philosophy than those who wrote later because as the period continued, writers could expect both American and British readers of political arguments to have become familiar with the fundamental grounds upon which those arguments rested.

Despite the fact that Otis expends much effort in the introduction to his *Rights of the British Colonies* on a discussion of political philosophy in order to state the most basic premises of American political thought, it is clear that his discussion is, in places, incomplete. We have noted his choice not to bother to answer the critics of the doctrine that all just governments must be based upon contract. There are other important theoretical issues that Otis treats as even less controversial. He grants without argument that "property has a precarious existence antecedent to government" and that "the security of property is one end of government." Similarly, he writes of

9. *JO*, 426.
10. *Ibid.*

the "natural equality and liberty of mankind" as the premise from which the truth of the original compact theory follows, but without presenting evidence for the truth of the premise. Furthermore, he says that "the experience of ages has proved that such is the nature of man, a weak, imperfect being, that the valuable ends of life cannot be obtained without the union and assistance of many" and that they cannot live together without fighting, so government is needed to arbitrate between them.[11] That the government once established must concern itself with the good of the whole may be a truism, but the claim that pursuing that good means providing for the security of life, liberty, and property is a contention that is arguable. These discussions of the state of nature and the reasons human beings choose to enter society are presented without argument or demonstration.

These premises about the natural state of human beings—their rights, their equality, and their liberty—form the foundation of the natural rights philosophy upon which Otis bases his argument against British taxation. Yet they are premises presented without careful argument. Otis sought to use the most basic ground about the goals of politics in order to make clear his objections to British policy, so why did he not state that ground in more detail? Why not present the evidence for the natural equality and liberty of mankind? Why not demonstrate, instead of simply mention, the argument that private property has a natural existence antecedent to the establishment of civil society (the argument from which the right to property is derived)? There is no doubt that he was aware of the arguments, for the points come from John Locke's *Essay Concerning the True Original, Extent, and End of Civil Government.* Otis' familiarity with that work is abundantly clear from his writing, for he refers to Locke in a substantive manner eight times in the pamphlet. Otis treats these important points as given, as self-evident, because it was sensible to do so. His political argument depends for its persuasiveness upon a particular set of theoretical premises, but if his readers know and accept those premises, it is hardly necessary to dwell on the arguments behind them. He did not need to preach to the converted about natural rights and the duty of government to secure them. His theory was neither new nor controversial to his readers in England and America. His point, then, was not to elucidate a new philosophy but to show how an accepted philosophy bears on a particular and immediate political issue.

11. *JO*, 422, 425.

Having explained the natural right of the individuals in a society to decide for themselves what form of government they will have, Otis considers some information from the "law of nature and reason" about the structure of government. The powers of government are of two kinds, executive and legislative. Nature places those powers in the hands of the whole body of the people, who then must decide how the powers are to be administered. If the powers remain in the people, they must be administered by the majority. As communities grow, however, it becomes impossible for the whole body of the people to assemble to conduct society's affairs. Thus arises the need for representation and for deciding how the various powers of government ought to be distributed among representatives. Otis writes that "the grand political problem in all ages has been to invent the best combination or distribution of the supreme powers of legislation and execution. Those states have ever made the greatest figure, and have been most durable, in which those powers have not only been separated from each other but placed each in more hands than one or a few."[12] The constitution that comes closest to solving this problem perfectly, continues Otis, is the British. His discussion of the origin and end of government thus becomes a celebration of the British constitution.

To confirm the excellence of the British constitution, Otis demonstrates that it was indeed created by contract, as he has shown all just governments must be. The government of Britain was created by a convention after the abdication of James II. Although the whole people did not consent actively to the new government, they had ample opportunity to register their approval both at the time and since. "There was neither time nor occasion to call the whole people together. If they had not liked the proceedings it was in their power to control them, as it would be should the supreme legislative or executive powers ever again attempt to enslave them." What the convention did was establish a government that would protect the people's liberties, as Otis has explained is the natural end of government. "The present establishment founded on the law of God and of nature," he writes, "was began by the Convention with a professed and real view in all parts of the *British* empire to put the liberties of the people out of the reach of arbitrary power in all times to come."[13]

In the course of explaining the origin and excellence of the British

12. *JO*, 428.
13. *JO*, 429, 430.

constitution, Otis discusses an aspect of natural rights political philosophy that was to become very important for the Americans in succeeding years. The power of government, he says, is *"originally* and *ultimately* in the people," and "they never did in fact *freely,* nor can they *rightfully* make an absolute, unlimited renunciation of this divine right." When government abuses its power, when it goes beyond the limits set for it by the people in the original compact, when it stops protecting the rights of the people and begins endangering them, the people have the right to reclaim their power and reestablish government so that it will do what it ought. This is what the British people did in 1688 and what they could have done again, and would have done again, had the convention not established a good government to replace the arbitrary one of James II. "The people will bear a great deal before they will even murmur against their rulers; but when once they are thoroughly roused and in earnest against those who would be glad to enslave them their power is *irresistible.*"[14]

Otis closes his introduction with two long quotations from Locke's *Second Treatise of Civil Government* confirming the conclusion that the people have *"a supreme power to remove, or alter, the legislative when they find the legislative act contrary to the trust reposed in them."*[15] Two things about Otis' discussion of the right to revolution are worthy of note. First is the fact that he discusses the right, which he knows follows from the theory of natural rights that he has explained. Second, he mentions the right to revolution not in connection with American complaints against British rule but in order to establish the legitimacy of British rule. Otis' introduction proceeds from a discussion of the theoretical basis of good government to the conclusion that, as a practical matter, the British government is good because it is established according to the rules of God and nature.

Otis follows his introduction with two short sections on colonies and the natural rights of colonists. Having explained that just governments originate in consent and have as their purpose the security of individual rights, he is now interested in determining whether the same can be said for the government of colonies, or whether colonies and their governments must operate according to principles different from those that apply to ordinary political institutions.

After noting that there is little literature on the subject and that

14. *JO,* 424, 429.
15. *JO,* 434 (Otis' emphasis).

the most useful authority on the problem of colonies and the natural rights of colonists is John Locke, Otis concludes that the rights of human beings are unaffected by the fact that they might be living in colonies rather than in the mother country. The premise of his argument is simple: "In order to form an idea of the natural rights of the colonists, I presume it will be granted that they are men, the common children of the same Creator with their brethren of Great Britain." Human beings by their very humanity are born to liberty. They renounce a certain, well-defined portion of that liberty in choosing to join civil society. However, by becoming members of society, Otis writes, the colonists "have not renounced their natural liberty in any greater degree than other good citizens, and if 'tis taken from them without their consent they are so far enslaved."[16]

Otis' insistence that people who have their liberty taken away without their consent are enslaved is interesting in that it occurs three paragraphs after he has discussed the institution of chattel slavery. In explaining the natural freedom of human beings, Otis decries the injustice of slavery: "Nothing better can be said in favor of a trade that is the most shocking violation of the law of nature, has a direct tendency to diminish the idea of the inestimable value of liberty, and makes every dealer in it a tyrant, from the director of an African company to the petty chapman in needles and pins on the unhappy coast. It is a clear truth that those who every day barter away other men's liberty will soon care little for their own."[17] Slavery, he continues, brutalizes both master and slave. It makes both of them less than human because the fundamental human right of liberty—of making one's own choices and working for one's own purposes—is denied by one and denied to the other.

Government, it seems, also dehumanizes people when it acts without their consent and limits their freedom by doing things that it has not the authority, granted by that consent, to do. The slave's master and the arbitrary governing official commit the same offense against the law of nature. The chattel slave and the subject of an arbitrary government have been dehumanized in the same way, if not to the same degree. "No government," wrote Otis in 1762, "has a right to make hobby horses, asses, and slaves of the subject; nature having made sufficient of the two former, for all the lawful purposes of man, from the harmless peasant in the field, to the most refined

16. *JO*, 436, 438, 440.
17. *JO*, 439.

politician in the cabinet, but none of the last which infallible [infallibly] proves they are unnecessary."[18] The right to have one's liberty respected by government is natural, belonging to all human beings. In this respect, then, the rights of colonists do not differ from the rights of other subjects.

The longest part of the *Rights of the British Colonies* is Otis' application of the principles he developed in the first three parts to the political situation confronting the colonies and Great Britain. In this section, two themes predominate. It is not surprising, given John Adams' estimation that Otis was the principal founder of the Revolution, that one of those themes should be the injustice of Parliament's legislation attempting to tax the Americans. What is surprising is the other major theme: Otis claims that Parliament is the supreme legislature throughout the realm and that the Americans are properly subject to its laws.

The political purpose of Otis' pamphlet is to argue against the Sugar Act and, to a lesser extent, against the future passage of a stamp tax on the American colonists. Otis' argument is that such measures violate colonial rights because they are designed to take the Americans' money in order to help satisfy the London government's need for income. He bases his argument on "our rights as men and as freeborn subjects," not on the rights guaranteed in the charters that many of the colonies had with Great Britain. Those charters seem to be relatively unstable and uncertain, according to Otis, since they might be revoked by Parliament at any time. Applying his argument on the natural rights of colonists to the British colonists in particular, Otis writes that "every British subject born on the continent of America or in any other of the British dominions is by the law of God and nature, by the common law, and by act of Parliament (exclusive of all charters from the crown) entitled to all the natural, essential, inherent, and inseparable rights of our fellow subjects in Great Britain."[19]

Otis argues that in the history of the world the British government is the one that is closest to perfection in satisfying the requirements of nature. There are provisions in the constitution of that government that secure to people their natural rights. These "first principles of law and justice," which are "the great barriers of a free state and of the British constitution in particular," require that government not be arbitrary, that it govern by stated laws, that the end of those laws

18. Tudor, *James Otis*, 125.
19. *JO*, 444.

be the good of the people, and that taxes not be levied on the people without their consent in person or through representatives.[20]

The right to consent to taxation is derived from the natural right to property. "In a state of nature," writes Otis, "no man can take my property from me without my consent: if he does, he deprives me of my liberty and makes me a slave. If such a proceeding is a breach of the law of nature, no law of society can make it just."[21] The right to property is connected to the more comprehensive right to liberty. If property is not secure, then people do not have the freedom to choose how they will live. They become the slaves of those who control their property. Nature thus demands that government seek the security of private property, and the British constitution enforces this demand from nature by requiring that all taxes be granted by the people and not simply taken at the pleasure of arbitrary governors.

It follows from this discussion that Parliament violates the British constitution and the laws of nature when it levies a tax on the American colonists. This is true because the colonists are not represented in Parliament. The only legislatures that have the authority to tax the Americans are the colonial legislatures, in which they are represented. Otis notes that some in England make a distinction between internal taxes—taxes laid on land and the things on it for the purpose of raising revenue—and external taxes, duties on trade. They argue that Parliament may not lay internal taxes on the colonists because the colonists are not represented in Parliament; but they also insist that Parliament may levy external taxes on the Americans because Parliament is responsible for regulating the trade of the whole empire, and a duty levied on an article of trade is a means to accomplish this end. Otis will not allow the distinction. If Parliament may levy a tax on imported molasses, "why may not the Parliament lay stamps, land taxes, establish tithes to the Church of England, and so indefinitely? I know of no bounds."[22]

This is not to deny Parliament's authority to regulate the trade of the empire. Otis grants that it has the right to do so but only by prohibiting certain kinds of trade, not by taxing the trade of the Americans: "But though it be allowed that liberty may be enjoyable in a comfortable measure where *prohibitions* are laid on the trade of a kingdom or province, yet if *taxes* are laid on either *without* consent,

20. *JO*, 446.
21. *JO*, 447.
22. *JO*, 451.

they cannot be said to be free. This barrier of liberty being once broken down, all is lost. If a shilling in the pound may be taken from me against my will, why may not twenty shillings; and if so, why not my liberty or my life?"[23] The issue, then, is not what is taxed, but that human beings lose control of their property and with it their liberty when their property is at the disposal of a legislature in which they are not represented.

Otis concludes that the Sugar Act is unjust. It violates the Americans' natural rights to liberty and property, and their birthright as British subjects to be taxed only with their consent. The present injustice can be remedied only by repealing the tax. The injustice can be prevented in the future by ensuring that Americans are taxed only by legislatures in which they are represented. It would be equitable, writes Otis, to grant the colonists representation in Parliament.[24] Without that representation, the only taxation that can be just is taxation passed by the colonial legislatures, those in which the Americans are represented.

Otis' explication of the rights of British subjects concerning taxation is presented in a section that grants the utmost respect to the British Parliament. He criticizes the justice of the Sugar Act without criticizing Parliament. Otis' apparent ambivalence toward the authority of Parliament was noted by John Adams in 1818: "In his 'Rights of the Colonists Asserted and Proved,' though a noble monument to his fame, and an important document in the early history of the Revolution, there are, nevertheless, concessions in favor of authority in Parliament"—concessions that Adams thought inconsistent with Otis' earlier work.[25] Indeed, far from denying that Parliament had any authority over the Americans, as later American thinkers of the revolutionary period would do, Otis grants legitimate authority to Parliament in virtually all things, including, under certain conditions, taxation.

In the first part of his pamphlet, Otis argues that all just governments originate in the consent of the governed and that the British government was granted such consent at the time of the Glorious Revolution. Otis does not present a different or additional event in which the colonists gave consent to a government other than the British. This is why he does not base his claims for the colonists upon

23. *JO*, 461.
24. *JO*, 445.
25. *JA*, X, 296.

colonial charters, as others were to do. To Otis, the American colonists were Britons who had tacitly consented to be ruled by the government with the institutions, limits, and goals consented to in 1688.

There is no doubt that under the British constitution Parliament is the supreme legislature, with the authority to legislate for the good of the whole. This point Otis readily and frequently grants.[26] The colonial legislatures are to be considered merely "subordinate" legislatures. In order to understand this grant of supreme authority over the colonists to Parliament, however, we have to keep in mind that Otis believes Parliament to have supreme legislative power because the British constitution makes it that way. The British constitution does other important things as well: it declares that the end of government is the good of the whole, which is to be pursued by securing individual rights; further, it declares that those rights can be secure only if no one is taxed without his consent. Otis understood the Americans to be ruled by the British constitution, but to understand what that means for relations between the colonies and Parliament it is critically important to take the constitution as a whole. The authority it grants is real and binding on the Americans, but that authority must be considered in light of the limits the constitution puts on its use.

The problem appears more sharply in a pamphlet Otis published in 1765:

> No less certain is it that the Parliament of Great Britain has a just and equitable right, power, and authority to *impose taxes on the colonies, internal and external, on lands as well as on trade.* This is involved in the idea of a supreme legislative or sovereign power of a state. It will, however, by no means from thence follow that 'tis always expedient and in all circumstances equitable for the supreme and sovereign legislative to tax the colonies, much less that 'tis reasonable that this right should be practiced upon without allowing the colonies an actual representation. An equal representation of the whole state is, at least in theory, of the essence of a perfect parliament or supreme legislative.[27]

Here Otis makes the two points he derives from the British constitution: first, Parliament is the supreme legislative, and second, it is not equitable that people be taxed without being represented in the body that levies taxes. Certainly both points can be true at the same time, in which case Parliament's authority to tax is rightfully used only

---

26. *JO*, 442, 444, 454, 455, 456.
27. James Otis, *A Vindication of the British Colonies*, in Bailyn (ed.), *Pamphlets*, 555–56.

when the colonists are represented in it. The same point is made in *Rights of the British Colonies*: "When the Parliament shall think fit to allow the colonies a representation in the House of Commons, the equity of their taxing the colonies will be as clear as their power is at present of doing it without, if they please."[28] For Otis, Parliament is supreme, but its power can be rightfully used only within the bounds consented to at the time of the Glorious Revolution.

There is another perspective from which Otis' deference to Parliament should be considered. Otis states that the British government is the best in the history of the world at doing what governments ought to do. His desire, then, is not to reject that government but to encourage it to continue protecting the rights of individuals both in America and in the mother country: "Rescued human nature must and will be from the general slavery that has so long triumphed over the species. Great Britain has done much towards it: what a glory will it be for her to complete the work throughout the world!"[29]

In writing about the revolution against James II, Otis noted that the people would bear a great deal before they revolt. At the time he was writing, the Americans had not had to bear enough even to consider that course. All of Otis' discussion of the right to revolution in *Rights of the British Colonies* is in celebration of the Glorious Revolution that established British government on the principles of nature, not in connection with the American grievances against Parliament. Indeed, while Otis argues that Parliament has violated the rights of the colonists, he does not counsel resistance. Instead he writes of the colonists' "affection and reverence" for the mother country and of their "cheerful and ready obedience to her laws." Furthermore, with regard to the taxes he writes that "we should be justifiable in refusing to pay them, but must and ought to yield obedience to an act of Parliament, though erroneous, till repealed."[30]

Otis was convinced that the Sugar Act violated the natural rights of the colonists. He was also convinced that the British government was the one best suited to the task of securing for human beings their natural rights. His pamphlet was thus designed to persuade that excellent government to live up to its principles so that his and his fellow citizens' rights could be made secure.

28. *JO*, 465.
29. *JO*, 459.
30. *JO*, 442, 447.

TWO

Patrick Henry

✥

Patrick Henry's importance in the conflict between the Americans and the British can be seen throughout the revolutionary period, but it lies in particular in bringing about colonial resistance to the Stamp Act. This act, passed by Parliament in 1765, required that many documents—including newspapers, diplomas, deeds, documents pertaining to lawsuits, and even playing cards—would have to carry a special stamp indicating that a tax had been paid on them. Although the fees were relatively small, the Stamp Act greatly concerned the colonists because, much more clearly than the Sugar Act, it levied a colonial tax whose sole and direct purpose was to raise money for the British government. On May 29, 1765, Henry introduced into the Virginia House of Burgesses a series of resolutions he wished the house to accept in order to register its opinion that the Stamp Act constituted a serious violation of colonial liberty. Following a stirring speech by Henry, the house did indeed adopt five resolutions condemning the act, though they repealed the fifth on the next day. A few weeks later the Virginia Resolves were published in papers throughout the continent. These papers, however, published more than the four resolutions that remained passed, publishing seven instead and giving the reader the impression that all seven had been passed by the Virginia House of Burgesses.

Before the Virginia Resolves were passed and published in papers throughout the colonies, many of the colonies had sent remonstrances to London in an attempt to persuade Parliament that the act violated their liberties as well as harmed economic policy. But Parliament had refused to give the petitions a hearing. The colonists appeared to be ready to obey the Stamp Act, to allow it to go into effect despite their objections to it. The alternative to repeal that was being accepted, albeit grudgingly, by the Americans and their patriot leaders was obedience to the law. James Otis, far from calling for resistance, wrote that "it is the duty of all humbly, and silently, to acquiesce in the decisions of the supreme legislature."[1] What intervened to prevent colonial acquiescence to the Stamp Act was a great potent combination: Patrick Henry, the Virginia Resolves, and the publication of the longer version of those resolves throughout the colonies.[2] By the fall of 1765, before the Stamp Act was to go into effect on November 1, stamp riots were occurring in Boston and elsewhere on the continent; stamp distributors in many colonies had been forced to resign; and eight other colonies had passed resolutions similar to those reported from Virginia.[3] The Stamp Act never had the effect that George Grenville and the Parliament had intended.

Both at the time and since, the dramatic change in colonial attitude has been attributed to the Virginia Resolves. Governor Bernard of Massachusetts wrote: "Two or three months ago I thought that this people would submit to the Stamp Act. Murmurs were indeed continually heard, but they seemed to be such as would die away. The publishing the Virginia resolutions proved an alarm-bell to the disaffected." General Gage wrote from New York that "the resolves of the assembly of Virginia, which you will have seen, gave the signal for a general out-cry over the continent." Thomas Jefferson later recalled the circumstances and wrote that the passing of the Virginia Resolves "may be considered as the dawn of the revolution."[4] John Adams wrote to Patrick Henry that Henry merited "the glory with posterity, of beginning . . . this great revolution."[5]

It is unfortunate that Patrick Henry's speech to the House of Burgesses to persuade its members to adopt the resolves was not pre-

---

1. Edmund S. Morgan and Helen M. Morgan, *The Stamp Act Crisis* (Chapel Hill, 1953), 69; William Wirt Henry, *Patrick Henry* (3 vols.; New York, 1891), I, 65.

2. On the importance of the Virginia Resolves as a catalyst to the revolt against the Stamp Act, see Merrill Jensen, "Commentary," in Randolph G. Adams, *Political Ideas of the American Revolution* (3rd ed.; New York, 1958), 12; and Edmund S. Morgan, *The Birth of the Republic, 1763–89* (Chicago, 1956), 22.

3. C. A. Weslager, *The Stamp Act Congress* (Newark, 1976), 66, 51.

4. Henry, *Patrick Henry*, I, 99, 100; Stan V. Henkels, "Jefferson's Recollections of Patrick Henry," *Pennsylvania Magazine of History and Biography*, XXXIV (1910), 389.

5. *JA*, IX, 386. Earlier Adams gave the same honor to Otis (see *JA*, X, 317). It is not important for present purposes to wonder which leader Adams would have found more important had he been pressed to choose. What is important is that Adams testifies to the extensive influence of each during the revolutionary period.

served. However, it was not the speech but the resolves—and not the resolves that actually passed the House of Burgesses but the resolves as published in the papers—that stirred resistance to the Stamp Act. Those resolves are preserved, and in analyzing them we can learn something of importance about the political thought behind the American Revolution.

The first resolution is as follows:

> Resolved, That the first Adventurers, Settlers of this his Majesty's Colony and Dominions of Virginia, brought with them and transmitted to their Posterity and all other his Majesty's subjects since inhabiting in this his Majesty's Colony all the Priviledges and Immunities that have at any Time been held, enjoyed, and possessed by the People of Great Britain.[6]

This initial resolve refers to the citizens of Virginia as subjects of the king rather than as citizens of Great Britain. Nowhere in the resolves does the word "Parliament" appear. Although the resolves were written because of an act of Parliament and an opinion that the act violated colonial liberties, it is not restraints on the power of Parliament that the resolves speak of but restraints upon the king. The resolves do not even go so far as to recognize any authority on the part of Parliament to govern the colonies. Their purpose is to remind the king that Parliament does not have authority to govern the colonies in a particular area, and they seem to leave aside the question of whether Parliament might have rightful authority to legislate for the colonies in other cases.

This first resolve makes the point that, as subjects of the king, the colonists are entitled to enjoy certain privileges and immunities that belong to British subjects and that those rights are possessed by the Americans as fully as they would be were the Americans to have been born and residing in England. Indeed, the resolve states that the Americans are rightfully possessed of all privileges and immunities "that have at any Time" been possessed by the people of Great Britain. That is to say, the fact that a right of British subjects might be commonly abridged in England at the time of the writing of the resolves does not mean that the right is justly abridged either in England or in the colonies. The colonists are therefore within their rights to claim that such abridgment must cease.

The first resolve presents the first ground upon which the Virgin-

6. Unless otherwise noted, the Resolves are quoted from the Boston *Gazette*, July 1, 1765.

ians based their argument against the Stamp Act: it violates rights belonging to them as British subjects. The second ground upon which the colonists based their claim to exercise certain rights is described in the second resolve:

> Resolved, That by two royal Charters granted by King James the First the Colony aforesaid are declared entitled to all Priviledges and Immunities of natural born Subjects, to all Intents and Purposes, as if they had been abiding and born within the Realm of England.

The rights of the Americans, according to this statement, are guaranteed not only by the fact that they are British subjects but also by express contract with the king. The Virginians point to two charters in which they are promised the same treatment as that accorded subjects in Britain. This resolve rejects any contention that the colonists have to be treated differently because they are not living in the British Isles and asserts instead that the king has agreed to give the Virginians the same rights as other British subjects despite the fact that they live an ocean away from England.

Having argued that the Virginians are entitled to certain rights of British subjects both because they are British subjects and because their charters guarantee to them the continuance of those rights to them in America, the Resolves go on to describe the rights at issue with the Stamp Act. The third resolve reads:

> Resolved, That the Taxation of the People by Themselves, or by Persons Chosen by Themselves to Represent them, who can only know what Taxes the People are able to bear, or the easiest Method of Raising them, and must themselves be affected by every Tax laid upon the People, is the only Security against a Burthensome Taxation; and the distinguishing Characteristic of *British* FREEDOM; and, without which, the antient Constitution cannot exist.[7]

The right at issue here is the right of Britons to tax themselves, not to have taxes imposed upon them by some legislative body over which they have no control. This right, which is essential to protecting the more basic right to private property, the resolve declares to be of fundamental importance for Britons. Without its being protected, the British constitution is not present.

The third resolve does more than assert the right of British subjects

---

7. This resolution was not published in the Boston *Gazette*. The version used here was published in the Maryland *Gazette*, as quoted in Morgan and Morgan, *Stamp Act Crisis*, 95.

to tax themselves, for it explains why a body like Parliament cannot be allowed to lay taxes on the Americans. For two reasons taxes must be levied either by the people or by a body chosen by the people. The first argument is that the people must tax themselves because only they or their representatives are in a position to understand the particular circumstances in which the people live. Taxation can be just and reasonable only when it is based upon such an understanding. Without taxes being based upon an appreciation of the people's situation, the burden of taxation might be unfairly distributed; taxes might be unnecessarily destructive of private property; or they might be so high that they would unduly harm the people's prosperity.

The second argument in this resolution against parliamentary taxation concerns the prevention of tyranny. People must be taxed by themselves or their chosen representatives in order to ensure that taxes will not be levied merely to enrich the governors. When a representative assembly assesses taxes, it places those taxes on both the citizens and its own members. Since such legislators are "equally affected by such taxes," the people have a certain security that the legislators will not levy excessive taxes. This argument is also an argument against the doctrine of virtual representation as it applies to the Americans. That doctrine, used often in Britain to defend the justice of parliamentary taxation of the colonists, asserts that it does not matter whether each individual citizen participates in the actual choice of a legislative representative so long as some citizens participate in the choice of legislators, since all legislators—no matter who actually chooses them—are members of the same nation and seek the same national interest that affects and benefits all citizens. Whatever the validity of the doctrine of virtual representation for Britons living in England, the third resolution makes clear the falsity of the doctrine that Americans are virtually represented by the members of Parliament elected from England. Taxes levied by Parliament on the Americans are not also paid by subjects living in England; so there is no personal interest that might make members of Parliament unwilling to lay excessive taxes on the Americans, as there is in the case of Britons living in England.

Furthermore, the third resolution at least hints that the doctrine of virtual representation may not provide just or adequate representation in Parliament even for those living in England. Representation, the resolution asserts, must be actual enough for the representative to know the circumstances of his constituents so that the government may employ the easiest mode of taxation. The claim that justice demands taxes be passed only by representatives with such specific knowledge implies the need for a subject to be actually, rather than virtually, represented in the legislative body. Are the people of Manchester legitimately represented in the Parliament if they have no vote on any member of Parliament? Can the legislators who levy the taxes be sufficiently aware of the particular situations in Manchester to make the taxation just? The third Virginia Resolve implies that the answers are no.

In this context the assertion in the first resolve that the rights of British subjects remain rights that must be respected in the colonies even if they have come to be habitually denied in England becomes important. The assertion of the third resolve is that it is the fundamental right of British subjects to be actually represented in the body that passes tax legislation. Violations of that right—whether in the colonies or in England itself—are injustices of the most serious order.

The fourth resolution continues the argument that the colonists have the exclusive right to tax themselves. It reads:

> Resolved, That his Majesty's liege People of this his most ancient Colony have enjoy'd the Right of being thus govern'd, by their own assembly, in the Article of Taxes and internal Police; and that the same have never been forfeited, or any other Way yielded up, but have been constantly recogniz'd by the King and People of Great Britain.

The first three resolutions seek to ground the colonists' argument against the Stamp Act in traditional rights. This fourth resolution continues to emphasize the fact that the colonists are asserting nothing new or startling but rather the justice of a process that has been known and followed by the king, the colonists, and the people of Great Britain. Thus the resolution claims that the right to be taxed by themselves is one that the Virginians have always practiced. The right has existed not only in theory but in actual practice throughout the history of the colony; and not only has it existed in practice, but the right has been habitually respected by the kings and people of Great Britain. What is new in the present dispute, then, is not the colonists' assertion of their sole and exclusive right to tax themselves but Parliament's assertion that it may levy a tax upon the colonists. *NCW*

This fourth resolution, with its claim that the colonists have always enjoyed a freedom from Parliamentary taxation, raises an interesting question that became more important over the duration of the dispute between the Americans and the British over taxation. The problem was that Parliament had, in the past, appeared to tax the colonists without their consent through laying duties on things imported into the colonies. These duties, while often ignored and objected to on economic grounds, had not been objected to by the colonists in the same way they were objecting to the Stamp Act. The Americans had accepted parliamentary authority to assess duties in the regulation of trade, yet here the resolve claims that the colonists had never accepted a parliamentary authority to tax the Americans and that Parliament had never acted as if it had such an authority. The assertion must imply some distinction, not here developed, between duties on trade and taxes.

These resolutions are the four passed by the Virginia House of Burgesses. The fifth resolution, apparently passed by a mere one-vote margin but then repealed the following day after Henry had left Williamsburg, seems to be little more than a summary and conclusion. It reads as follows:

> Resolved Therefore that the General Assembly of this Colony, Together with his Majesty or his Substitutes, have, in their representative capacity, the only exclusive Right and Power to lay Taxes and Imposts upon the Inhabitants of this Colony, And that every Attempt to vest such Power in any other Person or Persons whatever, than the General Assembly aforesaid, is illegal, unconstitutional and unjust, and have a manifest Tendency to destroy British as well as American Liberty.

At first reading, it is not clear why this resolution should be more controversial than the others. In both form and content it is a conclusion that follows from the other four. Yet this resolution, according to Thomas Jefferson, prompted Peyton Randolph to exclaim, as he was leaving the house after the vote, "By God, I would have given 500. guineas for a single vote," because one more vote in opposition would have defeated the resolution. It was rescinded the following day in such a way that all record of its ever having been passed was removed from the journal of the House of Burgesses. On reflection, it appears that the strength of this resolution comes from its clarity. Unlike the others, it does not present a legal argument against the Stamp Act. Rather it presents a clear and bold statement that the Parliament is destroying freedom. The statement does not limit itself to the Stamp Act but says that any attempt to tax the Americans other than by their own assemblies is destructive of freedom, both British and American. As a biographer of Henry has written, the fifth resolution "amounted to a direct charge of tyranny and despotism against the British king, lords, and commons."[8]

The boldness of the fifth resolution consists in another of its aspects as well. The resolution is stated in such a way as to provide a logical bridge to yet another conclusion—the conclusion that the Americans are justified in resisting the British in order to secure their freedom from unconstitutional and unjust taxation. The fact that the fifth resolution provides the premise for a yet bolder statement is indicated by the sixth and seventh resolutions.

The House of Burgesses passed five resolutions and then repealed the fifth. But when the event was reported in other colonies, seven resolutions were printed. It appears that the sixth and seventh resolutions were in Henry's possession during the debate in the house but that either he did not introduce them after the close vote on the fifth or they may have been debated but defeated.[9] The effect of the Virginia Resolves cannot be appreciated without understanding the sixth and seventh resolutions. The sixth reads:

> Resolved, That his Majesty's liege People, the Inhabitants of this Colony, are not bound to yield Obedience to any Law or Ordinance whatever, designed to impose any taxation whatsoever upon them, other than the Laws or Ordinances of the General Assembly aforesaid.

This resolution follows logically from the fifth, and with this fact in mind it is easier to appreciate the controversial nature of the fifth. The Americans have a right not to be taxed by any body in which they are not represented. Parliament thus has no right to tax them, and any attempt by Parliament to do so involves the assertion of an unconstitutional power. Therefore, should Parliament attempt to tax them, the Americans are not obliged to obey the statute levying the tax. The sixth resolution presents a clear call, not yet for resistance of an active sort, but for the passive resistance of not paying the stamp tax.

There is some uncertainty about which of the three resolutions—called here the fifth, sixth, and seventh—was actually the one passed by the House of Burgesses and rescinded the following day. In the copy of the resolves kept by Henry himself, that resolution is the fifth

8. Henkels, "Jefferson's Recollections," 389; William Wirt, *The Life of Patrick Henry* (New York, 1903), 66.

9. See Morgan and Morgan, *Stamp Act Crisis*, 95–97; also Robert Douthat Meade, *Patrick Henry: Patriot in the Making* (Philadelphia, 1957), 171–72. There is some uncertainty as to whether Henry himself actually wrote the sixth and seventh resolutions (see Meade, *Patrick Henry*, 169).

as listed above, but there is other evidence to suggest that Henry's recollection may have been incorrect.[10] The question is an interesting one but need not be answered for the purpose of understanding the political argument from the resolves that made people more willing to act against the Stamp Act. The resolves as published, all seven of them, are what is of prime importance. The final three all share a tone that is slightly different from the tone of the first four. While the first four resolves are of a more academic or descriptive tone, the final three are more inflammatory: they suggest that the argument of the first four resolves would justly lead to action on the colonists' part to resist the Stamp Act.

In this the seventh resolution goes further than the sixth or the fifth:

> Resolved, That any person who shall, by speaking or writing, assert or maintain that any Person or Persons, other than the General Assembly of this colony, have any Right or Power to impose or lay any Taxation on the People here, shall be deemed an Enemy to his Majesty's Colony.

This resolution surely is the boldest of all, for not only does it assert that Virginians who defend a parliamentary right to tax Americans are enemies of their homeland, it also implies that the Parliament, and perhaps even the king, is an enemy of Virginia. The implication is that they are enemies not for passing the Stamp Act but simply for asserting the right to tax the Americans, that is, for asserting the existence of a tyrannical power. While this seventh resolution does not state overtly the right or duty to resist the Stamp Act, it does seem at least to imply that right. For one surely has the right as well as, under some circumstances, the duty to resist an enemy, and the resolution manifestly brands the supporters of the act as enemies. Thus the resolution implies not only the right not to obey acts that are destructive of freedom but also the right to resist attempts to enforce such acts.

The argument of the first four of the Virginia Resolves was not a new one. Indeed, it appears that one reason many opposed the resolves in the House of Burgesses was not because of their content but because their content was so similar to the petition that the house had sent to Parliament the year before. John Adams later wrote: while the resolves did "great honor" to Henry and to Virginia, "these re-

---

10. Morgan and Morgan, *Stamp Act Crisis*, 96–97; Henkels, "Jefferson's Recollections," 398.

solves made no alteration in the opinion of the colonies, concerning the right of parliament to make that act [the Stamp Act]. They expressed the universal opinion of the continent at that time; and the alacrity with which every other colony, and the congress at New York, adopted the same sentiment in similar resolves, proves the entire union of the colonies in it, and their universal determination to avow and support it." The question thus arises as to what it was in Henry's resolutions that "lighted the fuse of resistance" in the colonies.[11]

The answer lies in the fact that Henry's resolves did more than explain the grounds for the colonial opinion that the Stamp Act was an unconstitutional violation of liberties critical to the lives of British subjects. Jefferson writes that in the year preceding Henry's resolutions, the petition passed by the House of Burgesses had stated the argument against parliamentary taxation "in a more conciliatory form." An author in the Boston *Gazette* praised Virginia for its "Spirited Resolves." In another edition of that same paper, an author asked this question: "What is the reason than that these Rights and Liberties, when they have been threatened and attack'd, are not as boldly asserted by every government in America as by Virginia?"[12]

Before the Virginia Resolves, statements by colonial assemblies in opposition to the Stamp Act had had the character of petitions—requests that the British government not pass the Stamp Act because of the harm it would pose to colonial liberty.[13] Henry's resolutions seem addressed more to the Americans than to the British government. They suggest strongly not only that the Stamp Act violated colonial rights—something that, as Adams noted, was already widely believed—but that the Americans ought to resist that violation. Henry's resolutions follow through the logic of the argument that Parliament has no legitimate authority to tax the colonists. If Parliament has no such authority, then taxing the colonists is a tyrannical act that the colonists are not bound to obey, an act that could be supported only by enemies of the colony. The special effect of Henry's resolves, then, lies in the fact that they are not "conciliatory" but a "spirited" and "bold" argument that the colonists' liberties are real, important, and not to be allowed to be abridged.

11. Henkels, "Jefferson's Recollections," 389; Morgan and Morgan, *Stamp Act Crisis*, 93; *JA*, IV, 50; Weslager, *Stamp Act Congress*, 99.

12. Henkels, "Jefferson's Recollections," 389; Boston *Gazette*, July 8, 15, 1765.

13. Wirt, *Life of Patrick Henry*, 54.

It is interesting to note that Patrick Henry, the great orator, made his most important contribution to the American cause not with an inspiring speech but with a series of relatively dry resolutions that served to recall to his fellow citizens the meaning of their principles. Henry preserved a copy of the five Resolves passed by the Virginia House of Burgesses for posterity. On the back of that copy he wrote a short account of the history and importance of the resolves: "After a long and warm contest, the resolutions passed by a very small majority, perhaps of one or two only. The alarm spread throughout America with astonishing quickness, and the ministerial party were overwhelmed. The great point of resistance to British taxation was universally established in the colonies."[14] Henry was correct in saying that the great accomplishment of his resolves was to establish the "point of resistance to British taxation." The point was established not because the resolves presented any new argument against that taxation but because they reminded Americans of their principled argument against taxation and urged them to take that argument and its implications seriously.

14. *Ibid.*, 64.

THREE

John Dickinson

❧❀❧

John Dickinson is most frequently remembered as the leading opponent of American independence at the Continental Congress in 1776. Only his abstention on July 2 prevented Pennsylvania from voting against independence. When Dickinson is connected to the revolutionary cause at all, it is usually as the "conservative revolutionary": the man sympathetic to the American position but unwilling to act decisively to change it.[1] Although Dickinson was indeed opposed to independence at the particular time it came, he was certainly not opposed to independence in theory. Quite the opposite of "conservative revolutionary" is true, for while in 1776 Dickinson believed that the time for revolution was not ripe because the American colonies were not prepared to win a battle against the mother country, there was no American more responsible for American independence than John Dickinson. His opposition to independence in 1776 was a thing far less important in American history than his arguments in the previous decade about the rights of Americans and the limits on the British parliament.

Dickinson is known as the "Penman of the Revolution" because of his clear, well-argued, and very influential writings of the revolutionary period. Until 1776, his writings had made him better known by his fellow countrymen than any American except Benjamin Franklin. His biographer writes: "By 1773 John Dickinson was recognized as the leading champion of American liberty throughout the colonies. His writings and his every declaration earned him that place."[2]

1. See, for example, the title of the most recent biography of Dickinson: Milton E. Flower, *John Dickinson: Conservative Revolutionary* (Charlottesville, 1982).
2. *Ibid.*, 69, 100

41

Not the volume but the clarity and quality of his writings earned him that place. Once Dickinson's comments on the Townshend Acts brought him to the attention of his fellow colonists, his thoughtfulness and his ability to clarify difficult issues of political thought in order to make them applicable to the American situation made him not only the leading spokesman for the American position but also a leading creator of that position. Not only could he write well the things that his fellow citizens were thinking, but he was also able to help them understand what they ought to be thinking in addition to what they ought to be doing to ensure the health of their political community.[3]

Dickinson's conservatism, though, is easily overstated. It is certainly true that he opposed independence in 1776 and that he continued to pursue reconciliation while the bulk of the Continental Congress had turned away from that course. It is also true, however, that Dickinson's opposition to independence in 1776 was not based upon any principled belief that the colonial position was wrong or that the British government had the right to do the things it had done that had readied his colleagues to vote for independence. Dickinson never took the British side against the Americans. His opposition to independence in 1776 was based upon an argument not that it would be wrong to seek independence but that in a war for independence the Americans, who would have right on their side, would lose to the might of the British.[4]

Dickinson, then, was at base a revolutionary, and a very important one, whose conservatism at the time the Revolution began was real but not fundamental. More than anything else, he was a man deeply committed to liberty. While his pragmatism of 1776 must be noted and understood, it should not be allowed to cast a shadow on the critically important role he played as a leader of American revolutionary thought. Careful analysis of Dickinson's political arguments from the era of the Revolution indicates that of the major revolutionary leaders Dickinson was the most radical in his thought. If to be conservative is to place emphasis on the importance of sources of order in the community—sources of order like institutions of government, constitutions, and precedents—then Dickinson was less conservative, more radical, than the other major revolutionaries.

3. See Pauline Maier, *From Resistance to Revolution* (New York, 1972), xiii.
4. David L. Jacobson, *John Dickinson and the Revolution in Pennsylvania, 1764–1776* (Berkeley, 1965), 113–14; Flower, *John Dickinson*, 122, 164.

One among Dickinson's writings is the most important; indeed, it is the most important political writing of the revolutionary period. Between December, 1767, and February, 1768, Dickinson wrote his *Letters from a Farmer in Pennsylvania to the Inhabitants of the British Colonies*. Commentators agree that these letters are the most acute analysis of the American political situation of the era.[5] The letters were written for a Pennsylvania newspaper but soon were republished in all but four of the papers in the thirteen colonies and subsequently appeared in pamphlet form. No political work was as widely read or as enthusiastically received in the American colonies until Thomas Paine's *Common Sense*. "It ran through the Colonies like wild fire, causing an enthusiasm which led Town Meetings, Societies, and Grand Juries to vote thanks to the author; which made him a toast at public dinners, and the subject of laudatory articles and poems in the press."[6] The *Farmer's Letters* are a critical source to understand if one seeks to comprehend the political thought of the American Revolution. For that reason, my discussion of John Dickinson's revolutionary thought will concentrate upon a careful analysis of those letters.

Dickinson writes that the purpose of the *Farmer's Letters* is "to convince the people of these colonies, that they are at this moment exposed to the most imminent dangers; and to persuade them immediately, vigorously, and unanimously, to exert themselves, in the most firm, but most peaceable manner, for obtaining relief."[7] The source of this great danger was the Townshend Acts. In 1766, in response to the pressure from a colonial boycott of British goods as a protest to the Stamp Act, Parliament had repealed the offending tax. But with the repeal of the Stamp Act Parliament passed the Declaratory Act, asserting its right to legislate for the colonies in any way it might choose. Thus, Parliament had done what the Virginia Resolves had said was just, but it had not agreed with the principled argument of those resolutions. According to Parliament, the Stamp Act was repealed because it was expedient to do so and not because it was just to do so.

In 1767 Parliament passed the Townshend Acts with the same purpose as had been behind the Stamp Act: gaining some revenue for

5. See Gordon S. Wood, *The Creation of the American Republic, 1776–1787* (Chapel Hill, 1969), 38–39; and Bernard Bailyn, *The Ideological Origins of the American Revolution* (Cambridge, 1967), 215.

6. Bailyn, *Ideological Origins*, 100; *JD*, 279.

7. *JD*, 324.

the British treasury from the American colonists. The Townshend Acts differed from the Stamp Act, however, in that they did not place a direct tax upon the citizens of the colonies but levied indirect taxes in the form of customs duties on items including paper, glass, and tea, to be paid at American ports. Although American consumers would surely end up paying the taxes, the Townshend Acts appeared much more like acts for regulating trade than had the stamp tax and, accordingly, less dangerous to the welfare of the colonists than the Stamp Act. This more benign appearance worried Dickinson, for he knew that the Townshend Acts represented a severe threat to American liberty, but he feared that his fellow citizens would be unlikely to understand that threat and unlikely to act to head it off. The problem for Dickinson was all the greater in that the duties laid by the Townshend Acts were not very large: the financial pain they would cause the colonists would not be so great as, alone, to make the Americans willing to sacrifice in order to secure the repeal of the acts. He writes that "nations, in general, are not apt to *think* until they *feel*; and therefore nations in general have lost their liberty."[8] The duties set by the Townshend Acts might not be so large as to make enough Americans feel harmed, so Dickinson wrote the *Farmer's Letters* to make them understand the harm that these acts posed to American liberty.

Dickinson's theme in the *Farmer's Letters* is not primarily the threat to property but the more comprehensive threat to liberty. The most immediate threat from the Townshend Acts was surely a threat to property—the property that might be taken from the Americans through taxes. But Dickinson sees that the fundamental issue is liberty, not property, because he sees the right to private property as important primarily because property is a means to liberty: "we cannot enjoy Liberty without Property." Property must be secure in order for freedom of action to be secure. Moreover, while liberty is the dominant political theme for Dickinson, his argument is that liberty is important because it is essential for the most comprehensive of human goals, human happiness.[9]

Like most of the other major American political authors of the revolutionary period, Dickinson appears to have believed that the meaning of liberty and its critical importance for human happiness were things that were clear to his audience. Thus, the reader finds in the *Farmer's Letters* no sustained, thematic discussion of the topic.

8. *JD*, 389.
9. *JD*, 416, 202, 262, 353.

These issues, however, may not be so clear to later readers of Dickinson, and in order to appreciate fully his argument about the threat posed by the Townshend Acts, it is crucial to have an understanding of the things Dickinson believed to be at stake. Fortunately, much can be drawn from Dickinson's writings to clarify his understanding of liberty. Liberty is, for Dickinson, essential to human happiness. Because it is essential for human happiness, liberty is something that is natural to human beings: human beings by nature love liberty and human beings by nature possess liberty, although it is certainly possible that the exercise of such a natural right may not be enjoyed by some.[10]

What Dickinson believes is natural is for human beings to have the freedom from outside control that allows them to determine their own lives. This freedom of self-determination is a right of human beings because without it they cannot realize their natures. Without liberty, the special dignity of human beings is lost. That dignity lies in the fact that human beings are rational creatures—creatures capable of deciding for themselves how they should act and not act. In the last of the *Farmer's Letters*, Dickinson challenges his fellow Americans to act in such a way that the world will be convinced "that YOU indeed DESERVE liberty, who so *well understand* it, so *passionately love* it, so *temperately enjoy* it, and so *wisely, bravely,* and *virtuously assert, maintain,* and *defend* it." Elsewhere, he writes to the king that the moderation of the Americans proves that they are deserving of liberty.[11] Liberty, then, is connected to rational behavior. It rightly belongs to human beings because they are rational. That is to say, the freedom to control oneself ought to be exercised by human beings because they have the capacity for self-control through reason. It is not simply acting as a rational human being would act that is important for humanity; what is important, if a person is going to be fully human, is having the freedom to decide—and actually deciding—how a rational human being ought to act.

British government had given the colonists the habits of liberty and of using liberty responsibly. Dickinson writes that had the colonists been unused to liberty, they would have developed neither the taste for it nor the understanding of its importance for humanity. "Had our Creator been pleased to give us existence in a land of slavery," he writes, "the sense of our condition might have been miti-

10. *JD*, 34, 39, 262, 353.
11. *JD*, 324, 390, 406, 460.

gated by ignorance and habit." People whose reason is undeveloped—people used to living according to the commands of others—possess the "stupid serenity of servitude" that leaves them content in the absence of the right of self-determination. That contentment, how-ever, is the contentment of a subhuman creature, for a genuine hu-man being is rational, and a rational human being cannot be content without the opportunity for self-control. Having been raised above the level of lesser beasts, Americans would commit the "highest crime against ourselves and our posterity" if they allowed liberty, and with it the dignity of being human beings, to slip or be taken away.[12]

"The first principles of government," Dickinson writes, "are to be looked for in human nature." Specifically, government is to be founded upon the understanding that liberty is essential for human happiness. A people who are to be in control of themselves must have some control of their own material resources, and so "no free people ever existed, or ever can exist, without keeping, to use a common, but strong expression, 'the purse strings,' in their own hands." A people who can be taxed without their consent are slaves, people whose lives are under the absolute control of those who control the material resources. The right of a people to decide what to grant to their gov-ernment in taxes, then, is a natural one, derived from an understand-ing of human nature. This right is also present in the British constitu-tion, but it depends upon that constitution not for its existence but merely for its confirmation. While Dickinson agrees with other American commentators that the right not to be taxed without con-sent is a right of Englishmen, he seems much less likely than other Americans to base his arguments against the Stamp Act or Towns-hend Acts upon constitutional grounds and more likely to appeal directly to natural rights, specifically, the natural right to liberty. Moreover, unlike other Americans, he consciously refuses to base his arguments against parliamentary taxation of the Americans upon the claim that charters granted to the American colonies guarantee to Americans the rights of British subjects (especially the right to be represented in the body that levies taxes). To speak of charters as the guarantors of liberty, he writes, would suggest that "all the liberties of the subject were mere favours granted by charters from the crown."[13] The liberty of human beings is theirs by natural right. It is

12. *PWD*, II, 24; *JD*, 373; *PWD*, I, 345.
13. *JD*, 388, 364, 357, 371, 195, 261.

good that that liberty is guaranteed by the British government, according to Dickinson, but he is always clear that whether that liberty were guaranteed by the government or not, it most clearly ought to be, so that the actions of the Americans should not be controlled by concerns about what the government allows or demands so much as by an understanding of what human happiness requires.

After we have considered the meaning and importance of liberty as a political goal for Dickinson, the next step in understanding his argument in the *Farmer's Letters* is to see how he believes the Townshend Acts presented a serious threat to Americans' liberty. The threat is threefold: a direct violation of American liberty involved in taxing the colonists without their consent; the possibility that the money raised through the taxes levied by the Townshend Acts would be used to restrict American liberty further; and the danger that the Townshend Acts would provide a precedent for far more oppressive parliamentary legislation in the future.

To Dickinson, the injustice of the Townshend Acts is identical to the injustice of the Stamp Act: they both levy taxes upon the Americans without their consent. In the *Farmer's Letters* Dickinson makes this point clearly by quoting from the resolutions passed by the Stamp Act Congress in 1765: "It is *inseparably essential to the freedom of a people*, and the *undoubted right* of *Englishmen*, that NO TAX be imposed on them, *but with their own consent*, given personally, or by their representatives." Supplies to the crown, the resolutions continued, are to be "free gifts of the people," and money is hardly a gift if a people has had no say in giving it. The Townshend Acts are wrong, then, for the simple and clear reason that they remove the Americans' liberty, which is essential to their humanity and happiness. "Every one of the most material arguments against the legality of the *Stamp-Act*, operates with equal force against the act now objected to."[14]

Yet there is an apparent difference between the Stamp Act and the Townshend Acts that this simple argument ignores. The Stamp Act taxed the colonists directly and for the sole purpose of acquiring money for the British government. The Townshend Acts placed a duty on certain imports and so taxed the colonists only indirectly as merchants would be forced to include the tax in the price of the imported items. The difference is important because although Parliament had never taxed the colonists directly before the Stamp Act, it

14. *JD*, 331, 336.

had always levied duties in the course of regulating trade. The Stamp Act had no clear precedent in America, but the Townshend Acts appeared to have precedent behind them.

Dickinson meets this objection squarely in the *Farmer's Letters*. He readily agrees that "the parliament unquestionably possesses a legal authority to *regulate* the trade of *Great-Britain*, and all her colonies."[15] The purpose of this power is to maintain the health of the whole empire and thus to contribute to the happiness of all the citizens of all the parts of the empire. However, there is a difference between regulating trade and levying taxes. Dickinson writes that there is a distinction to be made between different sorts of impositions laid upon the people by the government. One sort of imposition, duties to regulate trade, is laid for the purpose of maintaining the commercial health of the empire. The other sort of imposition, a tax, is laid for the purpose of gaining a revenue for the government.

The word *tax*, argues Dickinson, has a clear meaning that predates the need to use duties to regulate trade. By that meaning, a tax is "*an imposition on the subject, for the sole purpose of levying money.*"[16] Such impositions were always considered as gifts from the people to the crown to be used for securing the general welfare. The distinction made by some between "internal" and "external" taxes—with internal taxes being direct taxes upon the subject, like those levied under the Stamp Act, and external taxes those that have to do with the regulation of trade—is a distinction Dickinson finds to be meaningless. Taxes, as such, are not for the purpose of regulating trade but for raising money, and no matter what the form of the tax, it cannot be just unless it has been created by a body in which the subject is represented. All taxes are indeed internal, for all taxes are designed to take the subject's property and give it to the government.

Dickinson argues that the purpose of the Townshend Acts is clearly not to regulate trade but to raise a revenue. First, there is the fact that the acts create special duties on articles like paper and glass that the colonists must import from Great Britain. Certainly the Parliament has interest not in restraining such imports but only in taking advantage of the fact that the Americans have no choice but to continue to buy the imported goods. Second, and more decisive, there is the language of the act itself. Dickinson quotes the preamble, which begins by stating that "it is expedient THAT A REVENUE SHOULD

15. *JD*, 312.
16. *JD*, 329.

BE RAISED IN YOUR MAJESTY'S DOMINIONS IN AMERICA."[17] There could be no clearer indication that in passing the Townshend Acts Parliament has exceeded its legitimate authority and violated both natural and constitutional rights. Parliament boldly states that the purpose of the acts is not to regulate trade but to take the property of the colonists through a tax created without the consent of their representatives.

Dickinson feared that in addition to taking money from the colonists in violation of natural and constitutional rights, the British would use the money thus taken in ways that would further remove the Americans' liberty. He explains that according to the wording of the act, the revenue from the taxes levied under the Townshend Acts is to be used to pay for the administration of justice, for the upkeep of civil government, and for defense in the colonies. Traditionally, the money for these objects had been appropriated by the colonial assemblies, and Dickinson argues that it is critical to American liberty that the assemblies continue to control these items. With the purse strings in their own hands, the people "have a *constitutional check* upon the administration, which may thereby be brought into order *without violence:* But where such a power is not lodged in the *people,* oppression proceeds uncontrouled in its career."[18]

The judges in the colonies, as well as most of the colonial governors, served at the pleasure of the crown. The only tool available to the colonists to ensure some faithfulness on the part of these officials to the rights and interests of the colonists consisted in the fact that the governors and judges received their salaries from the colonial legislatures. The money from the taxes levied under the Townshend Acts was to be used, it appeared to Dickinson, to make governors and judges independent of the colonial legislatures and hence of the citizens of the American colonies who elected those legislatures. Such a move would eliminate the check that the Americans had against tyrannical actions by those officials. The people, writes Dickinson, "perfectly know *how much* their grievances would be regarded, if they had *no other* method of engaging attention, than by *complaining.*" Dickinson argues that the complete control of executive and judicial power in the colonies by the king ought to be a source of concern not only to the Americans but also to the British people and their Parliament. "The influence of the crown was thought by wise

17. *JD*, 316.
18. *JD*, 364.

men, many years ago, too great by reason of the multitude of pensions and places bestowed by it."[19] By creating new pensioners in the colonies, the Parliament would increase the influence of the crown at the expense of the power of the popular part of the British government, just as it would decrease the importance of the popular part of government in the American colonies.

The stated purpose of the Townshend Acts to provide money for defense in the colonies, especially when combined with the prospect of removing governmental officials from any colonial control, promised yet another grave danger to American liberty. "We may be chained in by a line of fortifications—obliged to pay for the building and maintaining them—and be told, that they are for our defence." Those soldiers, however, might actually be used to enforce the oppression of the colonists by officials over whom the colonists would have no control. "Is it possible," Dickinson asks, "to form an idea of slavery more *compleat*, more *miserable*, more *disgraceful*, than that of a people, where *justice is administered, government exercised*, and a *standing army maintained*, AT THE EXPENCE OF THE PEOPLE, and yet WITHOUT THE LEAST DEPENDENCE UPON THEM?"[20]

Dickinson is very concerned indeed that the money raised through the Townshend Acts will be used to alter decisively the colonial governments, just as he is genuinely concerned that the acts try to take the colonists' property without their consent. But the danger that worries him most is that the acts can create a precedent for the further removal of American liberty by the British. Dickinson's strong concern about this threat is caused by a realization that very oppressive measures can be passed with the acts as their precedent for legitimacy and also by a fear that his fellow citizens will not appreciate the great danger that will be posed by the acts if they are to be accepted as legitimate.

The taxes levied by the Townshend Acts, writes Dickinson, are actually quite small. Paying them will not create an insuperable financial burden for the colonists, and for that reason he fears that some might be inclined not to take the trouble to resist the law. Dickinson argues to his fellow citizens that such conduct would be deadly to freedom for the Americans. "I am convinced," he writes, "that the authors of this law would never have obtained an act to raise so trifling a sum as it must do, had they not intended by *it* to establish

19. *JD*, 365, 381.
20. *JD*, 366, 372.

a *precedent* for future use. To console ourselves with the *smallness* of the duties, is to walk deliberately into the snare that is set for us." The Townshend Acts, then, were designed to take the property of the colonists, but more so over the long term than over the short term. Dickinson attempts to convince his fellow Americans that the acts were meant to be "a bird sent out over the waters, to discover, whether the waves, that lately agitated this part of the world with such violence, are yet *subsided*." He goes so far as to say that "the late act of Parliament is *only* designed to be a PRECEDENT, whereon the future vassalage of these colonies may be established." His great challenge in the *Farmer's Letters* is to convince his fellow citizens to act to avoid a danger that they cannot yet feel but that must be addressed now, before the authority is well established to tax them without their consent. "We have a statute, laid up for future use, like a sword in a scabbard."[21] Dickinson's achievement in the *Farmer's Letters* was to make it clear to other Americans that the Townshend Acts were such a sword so that the Americans would act to remove the weapon before it could be used in more disastrous ways.

On the basis of his argument against the Townshend Acts, it is possible to appreciate the assertion that Dickinson is less conservative and more radical than other American revolutionaries. He leaves to the people more freedom to judge for themselves whether a government is worthy of support or whether there is good cause to resist it or to revolt against it. Ultimately, for Dickinson, legal, constitutional, and procedural issues are not decisive. The only thing that is decisive is whether a government, formally legitimate or not, does the best that can be done to help the people of the community secure their happiness.

Dickinson believes that government is to be evaluated according to whether it allows for human happiness. He argues that the primary contribution that government ought to make to human happiness is to provide for the security of liberty so that human beings will have the freedom for self-determination: "The happiness of the people is the end, and, if the term is allowable, we would call it the body of the constitution. Freedom is the spirit or soul." Anything that corrupts this spirit makes the good health of the body unachievable and is therefore contrary to the purpose of politics. Dickinson writes that "a tendency to diminish the happiness of the people, is a proof, that power exceeds a 'boundary,' beyond which it ought not to go." Since

21. *JD*, 355, 396, 395, 335.

the people's happiness is at stake here, the people themselves must make the judgment as to whether the government has crossed that boundary. "And have they not a right," Dickinson asks, "of JUDGING from the evidence before them, on no slighter points than their *liberty* and *happiness?*"[22]

This right of the people to judge is absolute. Their judgment may be that the best way to preserve their safety and happiness is to use violence to topple a government that is too dangerous. There are no easily recognized standards according to which the people make such a judgment; it is simply their responsibility to make an intelligent evaluation as to the best available means for them to protect themselves. What can be said with certainty for Dickinson is that the people must always be keenly aware of their responsibility for keeping their government faithful to its just purposes. They must be constantly vigilant, for "liberty, perhaps, is never exposed to so much danger, as when the people believe there is the least." Continual vigilance is essential, if a people is to preserve its liberty, because all governments are operated by human beings. It would be nice, Dickinson writes, to be able to assume that all measures of a government are good—and indeed people should assume that those who operate governments act with good intent until it is proven otherwise. But this certain fact remains: although Parliament may be the wisest and most just assembly on earth, "human wisdom and human justice partake of human frailties. Such is the lot of our nature—and to bestow the attributes of heaven on mortals, who to day are, and tomorrow are not, is the wildness of adulation."[23]

This likelihood that government will make mistakes, even disastrous ones, regardless of the motives of the governors, is even more marked in the British government as it operates over the American colonies. First, there is the fact that the British government is a mixed one, with the king and the lords vying with the people's representatives for power. In order to maintain freedom it is essential for the people to be always watchful lest that part of the government most responsible for the security of their liberty lose its influence to the ambition of the members of the other two branches of government. Second, there is the fact that the popular part of the government in Britain does not itself represent the American people. Dickinson writes that when legislators make laws "that are not designed to bind

22. *PWD*, I, 332, 333; *JD*, 348.
23. *JD*, 393, 265.

themselves, we cannot imagine that their deliberations will be as cautious and scrupulous, as in their own case."[24] Thus, extra care and vigilance is demanded of the American citizens lest things be done by the government in Britain to violate the Americans' liberties.

To say Dickinson argues that the people have an absolute right to judge whether the government is acting in harmful ways and to say the people must never relax in their vigilance toward the government and its actions with regard to their liberties is not to say Dickinson argues that the only safeguard against governmental tyranny is the watchfulness of the people. Like others, he makes the familiar argument that there ought to be constitutional barriers set up against tyranny and that those barriers ought to forestall the need for people to resist the government, whether lawfully or violently, in order to protect their liberties. Some confidence that the government will not act in ways that violate liberty appears to be necessary for the people to be really free: "For WHO ARE A FREE PEOPLE? Not *those*, over whom government is reasonably and equitably exercised, but *those*, who live under a government so *constitutionally checked* and *controuled*, that proper provision is made against its being otherwise exercised."[25] While he well appreciates the value of constitutional control both for preventing abuses of liberty and for giving the people sufficient confidence in the government to exercise their freedom, he does not assume that constitutional checks can be perfectly effective.

Because Dickinson knows that constitutional controls, though essential for preserving liberty, cannot always be depended upon to do the job, he argues that the people cannot rely upon legality or constitutionality as the standard by which to judge whether their liberty is threatened. The final standard is whether the government is tending to subvert their liberty and happiness. It is entirely possible, according to Dickinson, for a government under a good constitution to follow legal forms quite properly and still act in ways destructive of the end of government. "Nothing is more certain, than that the *forms* of liberty may be retained, when the *substance* is gone." It is also true that "all artful rulers, who strive to extend their power beyond its just limits, endeavor to give their attempts as much semblance of legality

24. *JD*, 350.
25. *JD*, 356. The notion of freedom discussed here is that contained in Montesquieu's definition of liberty—a tranquility of the mind arising from the opinion that one is safe. Dickinson used that definition, attributing it to Montesquieu, in a 1774 writing (*PWD*, II, 12).

as possible."²⁶ The people, then, cannot be satisfied that what appears legal is in fact permissible: they must guard not only the forms of liberty but also its reality.

Because Dickinson knows that the forms of liberty can be preserved while the reality of liberty is removed, he places a lesser emphasis upon constitutional and legal rights than others. An example of this point—curious in light of Dickinson's argument against the Townshend Acts—has to do with legal precedent. Dickinson argues that a precedent is not binding when it is bad. People may obey an unjust law out of ignorance, carelessness, or a calculation that obedience is the lesser evil, but "submission to unjust sentences proves not a *right* to pass them." Unhappy precedents do not "repeal the eternal laws of natural justice, humanity and equity." Yet Dickinson's greatest dread about the Townshend Acts is that they will be obeyed and used as a precedent for future restrictions of American liberty. His fear is not that such a precedent will be legally binding but that many will think of it as legally binding. Parliament would argue that its authority to tax the Americans without their consent had been admitted by the colonists when they obeyed the Townshend Acts, and many Americans would find the argument persuasive, "for millions entertain no other idea of the *legality* of power, than that it is founded on the *exercise* of power."²⁷

Dickinson's tendency to make judgments about the legitimacy of governmental actions by referring to the end of government rather than to the proper use of the means that have been established to meet those ends appears also in his arguments against the Townshend Acts. His argument against the Townshend Acts is that while the duties are placed upon imports into the colonies, the primary purpose of the acts is not to regulate trade but to tax the colonists. Since Parliament has no authority to tax the Americans, the laws are not legitimate. But how can one know whether a law that sets a duty on imports is passed to regulate trade or to raise a revenue? In the case at hand, Dickinson argues that the problem is not at all difficult, for in the preamble to the Townshend Acts Parliament states clearly that its purpose is to raise a revenue. In the long run, though, Dickinson's argument leaves no objective criteria that may be employed to determine whether an act is legitimate. Had he argued that Parliament may levy duties on trade but may not pass other kinds of taxes affect-

26. *JD*, 347, 346.
27. *PWD*, I, 395, 396; *JD*, 390.

ing the Americans, it would be easier to make a judgment as to the legitimacy of any given act. Because he knows, however, that the legitimate parliamentary authority to regulate trade can be used in illegitimate ways, he is not willing to grant a parliamentary authority to do all things relative to trade matters.

According to Dickinson's argument, a judgment about the legitimacy of any given act must be based upon a more subjective evaluation as to whether the act furthers or hinders the achievement of the end of government, not upon an evaluation as to whether it deals with trade or purely domestic matters. The people must make a judgment not about whether impositions are laid on trade but about whether the purpose of an imposition is to regulate trade or to raise money. They must make a judgment, based upon the appearance of the imposition, about the nature of the imposition: if it is to regulate trade, then the imposition is legitimate; but if it is to raise money, then the imposition is an illegitimate tax. "The *nature* of any impositions she may lay upon us may, in general, be known, by considering how far they relate to the preserving, in due order, the connection between the several parts of the *British* empire."[28] It is up to the people to examine a law and to determine whether the act seeks an end that Parliament may legitimately seek or one that it may not.

Dickinson's discussion of the Parliament's authority to bind the American colonists when regulating trade but not when levying taxes raises another issue that demonstrates his tendency to judge governmental actions by looking at whether they contribute to the end of government rather than by looking to constitutionality or technical legality. Most of the American political authors of the period took great pains to explain how it could be true that Parliament has the authority to make laws binding the colonists on some things, most especially trade, but not on others, like taxes. John Adams, for example, goes into careful detail in arguing that when the colonists came to America they were free agents with the right to make any sort of government they chose. They chose, Adams argues, to be governed by the king but not by Parliament. They then chose to contract with Parliament to allow the British legislature to make laws to regulate trade but no other sort of laws. Thus it is consistent for the Americans to claim that Parliament has no authority to tax them or to bind them with any laws except those that regulate the trade of the empire.

28. *JD,* 349.

It is very interesting to note that in the *Farmer's Letters* Dickinson engages in no similar discussion. He admits readily Parliament's authority to pass laws binding on the colonists with regard to the regulation of trade, but he engages in no analysis of the apparent difficulty in saying that Parliament may legislate for the colonists on some matters but not on others. Nor is Dickinson at all clear about where the authority to regulate trade comes from. At one point he suggests in passing that it might come from a "parental right." In other writings he suggests, again without extensive analysis, that Parliament's authority to regulate trade derives from tacit acquiescence by the colonists in such laws or from express contract.[29] But the issue is not very important, given Dickinson's understanding of politics. What is important to him is not the legal ground or lack of ground for authority but the question of whether a given piece of legislation will secure or threaten the people's happiness and liberty. Parliament may regulate trade, then, because when Parliament regulates trade it maintains a healthy empire, and a healthy empire contributes to the happiness of the Americans in a way that Parliament's taxing of the Americans cannot.

The fact that Dickinson encourages his fellow Americans to judge the legitimacy of Parliament's legislation on the radical basis of whether it furthers or hinders liberty and happiness rather than on the firmer and more tangible grounds of constitutionality or legality does not mean that he argues that whenever the people decide an act of government is bad they should revolt against the government. Dickinson is genuine when he speaks of the connection between American happiness and the colonies' remaining a part of the British empire. During the 1760s he had no desire for independence.[30] His call in the *Farmer's Letters* for the Americans to examine the requirements for their own happiness is a call for a careful and timely reaction to unjust parliamentary legislation in the hope that more radical action can be avoided in the future.

Dickinson's primary purpose in the *Farmer's Letters* is to explain the threat posed by the Townshend Acts to American liberty. When he calls for responses to that threat, he always calls for nonviolent, legal responses:

> Every government at some time or other falls into wrong measures. These may proceed from mistake or passion. But every such measure

29. *JD*, 344, 411; *PWD*, I, 386, 413.
30. *JD*, 261.

does not dissolve the obligation between the governors and the governed. The mistake may be corrected; the passion may subside. It is the duty of the governed to attempt to rectify the mistake, and to appease the passion. They have not at first any other right, than to represent their grievances, and to pray for redress, unless an emergence is so pressing, as not to allow time for receiving an answer to their applications, which rarely happens. If their applications are disregarded, then that kind of *opposition* becomes justifiable, which can be made without breaking the laws, or disturbing the public peace.

Frequently Dickinson urges his fellow citizens to follow this advice and to react to the Townshend Acts so as to "rectify the mistake," but to react with prudence and moderation: "The cause of *liberty* is a cause of too much dignity to be sullied by turbulence and tumult. It ought to be maintained in a manner suitable to her nature."[31]

Free human beings realize the importance of government for human happiness as well as the fact that no government can be perfect. They will, therefore, attempt to preserve government while trying to correct its mistakes. But in arguing this, Dickinson is not arguing that people *never* have the right or the responsibility to go beyond petition and other legal measures in addressing the injustice of government. "If at length it become UNDOUBTED, that an inveterate resolution is formed to annihilate the liberties of the governed, the *English* history affords frequent examples of resistance by force." Dickinson cannot say what conditions would have to be present for such revolution to be just, but he can say two things: there are conditions under which violent revolution would be just and prudent, and those conditions are extreme. "Perhaps it may be allowable to say generally, that it can never be justifiable, until the people are FULLY CONVINCED, that any further submission will be destructive to their happiness."[32]

Dickinson argues that the conviction that happiness will be destroyed by further obedience to the government must be complete because revolution is itself a great destroyer of happiness. "When appeal is made to the sword, highly probable is it, that the punishment will exceed the offence; and the calamities attending on war out-weigh those preceding it."[33] So that even when the people are genuinely convinced that their happiness cannot be reached under their present government, it remains possible that revolution will

31. *JD*, 325, 324.
32. *JD*, 325.
33. *JD*, 325–26.

bring about evils greater than will submission. Still, Dickinson argues, a people must do what it has to do to try to preserve liberty and happiness, and if they are indeed "fully convinced that any further submission will be destructive to their happiness," they can no longer submit.

Dickinson is very concerned in the *Farmer's Letters* that the danger of British tyranny be met early, before the problem might become so serious that violence would be the only remaining response. Such an eventuality would mean not only that the violations of liberty had become very severe but also that the rectification of the wrongs would be very painful. Once a dispute reaches the level of violence, he writes, people's passions tend to take over: "In quarrels between countries, as well as in those between individuals, when they have risen to a certain height, the first cause of dissension is no longer remembered, the minds of the parties being wholly engaged in recollecting and resenting the mutual expressions of their dislike. When feuds have reached that fatal point, all considerations of reason and equity vanish; and a blind fury governs, or rather confounds all things. A people no longer regards their interest, but the gratification of their wrath."[34]

Violence is destructive of happiness, then, because it excites people's passions to the point that the violence becomes more extreme and long-lasting than it needs to be to address the injustice. The fight itself rather than the grievance that gave rise to the fight becomes the focal point of people's thinking. The result is that considerations of prudence and caution disappear: "Wise and good men in vain oppose the storm, and may think themselves fortunate, if, in attempting to preserve their ungrateful fellow citizens, they do not ruin themselves. Their *prudence* will be called *baseness*; their *moderation* will be called *guilt*; and if their virtue does not lead them to destruction, as that of many other great and excellent persons has done, they may survive to receive from their expiring country the mournful glory of her acknowledgment, that their counsels, if regarded, would have saved her."[35]

The dangers involved in appeals to the sword are indeed great. Yet they are not so great as the evil of the loss of liberty. Dickinson's purpose in the *Farmer's Letters* is to warn both the British and the Americans that if violations of liberty like those that come with the Townshend Acts are allowed to continue and increase, the extreme

34. *JD*, 326–27.
35. *JD*, 327.

dangers associated with the use of violence will come: "Oppressions and dissatisfactions being permitted to accumulate—*if ever* the governed throw off the load, *they will do more.* A people does not reform with moderation."[36] As an example he cites the deposition of Charles I, who committed many small violations of liberty through extensions of prerogative. Dickinson writes that had each been stopped as it arose, the people would never have reached the point of overthrowing the monarchy. But the king refused to give up any of the powers the crown had usurped over the years. This multitude of oppressive acts gave rise to the end of the monarchy: "Acts, that might *by themselves* have been on many considerations excused or extenuated, derived a contagious malignancy and odium from other acts, with which they were connected. They were not regarded according to the simple force of each, but as parts of a system of oppression. Every one, therefore, however small in itself, became alarming, as an additional evidence of tyrannical designs."[37]

Because unjust acts were allowed to accumulate to the point where petition and other legal measures could not be effective, because the people allowed such acts to continue until they felt the effects of oppression, and because the king refused to abandon powers dangerous to liberty, violence erupted. The problem was that once events reached that stage, the people could not be moderated. Dickinson is arguing not that the people were wrong in perceiving the "tyrannical design" nor that they were wrong in acting against the king. Where they did overreact was in destroying the monarchy, and such passionate overreaction is the result of allowing restrictions of liberty to continue to the point where people no longer have an effective legal recourse with which to defend their liberty. At fault is the government for instituting oppressive acts. At fault also are the people for not opposing each small oppressive act as it arises and for waiting until they feel the oppression and the tyrannical design is in an advanced stage.[38]

In the *Farmer's Letters*, then, Dickinson is warning both his fellow

36. *JD*, 387.

37. *JD*, 387–88.

38. Bailyn argues that Dickinson's discussion of Charles I shows that Dickinson "forcefully conveyed the idea of conspiracy" and "understood so well the psychological and political effects of thinking in precisely these conspiratorial terms" (*Ideological Origins*, 145). But analysis of the passage indicates that Dickinson is not criticizing the fear of conspiracy. Indeed, he seems to have believed that such fear was well founded. Dickinson is criticizing the failure to act against the conspiracy earlier, for that failure led to the eventual violence and overreaction against monarchy.

colonists and the British of the risk involved in allowing the violation of liberty of the Townshend Acts to stand. His hope is to end the violations of liberty before they become so great that the people will overreact against the government that unjustly restricts their liberty. It is here that Dickinson's conservatism is to be found. He is opposed neither to change nor to the challenging of a government's authority. His is a conservatism that demands of the people that they make judgments as to when they must resist the government's actions and that they follow those judgments. Dickinson encourages constant vigilance in the name of individual rights, constant questioning of the uses of governmental authority, and a constant willingness to resist uses of the powers of government—whether those powers be technically legitimate or not—that might tend to endanger liberty. His first concern is never the conservation of political order; it is always the conservation of liberty. And when it came to conserving liberty, Dickinson was a radical thinker indeed. Dickinson himself makes the point clearly in a passage he contributed to the Continental Congress's *Declaration on the Causes and Necessity of Taking Up Arms* of 1775: "We are reduced to the alternative of choosing an unconditional submission to the tyranny of irritated ministers, or resistance by force.—The latter is our choice.—WE HAVE COUNTED THE COST OF THIS CONTEST, AND FIND NOTHING SO DREADFUL AS VOLUNTARY SLAVERY.—Honour, justice, and humanity, forbid us tamely to surrender that freedom which we received from our gallant ancestors, and which our innocent posterity have a right to receive from us."[39]

39. *PWD*, II, 40. On Dickinson's authorship of this passage, see Jacobson, *John Dickinson*, 96.

FOUR

Samuel Adams

Samuel Adams is renowned for stirring things up. He is given credit for being one of the more important men responsible for bringing the Americans to revolt against the British. He comes down to us as the "Pioneer in Propaganda," the man whose words led Americans to revolt.[1] Rarely, however, do we wonder about the meaning of his words. Adams' skills as politician and publicist are so celebrated that the fact that he wrote and spoke has come to be seen as the only fact of importance. Little attention is given to the content of his writings and speeches. But was Samuel Adams simply a rabble-rouser—a mere propagandist—or was he a statesman with arguments to explain the justice of his and his fellow citizens' actions against Great Britain? Certainly anyone who would seek to understand the causes of the American Revolution ought to be curious about the reasons for Samuel Adams' advocacy.

The reason for the general neglect of the content of Samuel Adams' political rhetoric may stem from his reputation. For years historians have painted a picture of Adams that suggests that there is no careful political thought to be found in his writings.[2] Adams' most influential biographer characterizes him as a man who would "shriek 'oppression' and 'tyranny,'" but whose "sincerity is open to question."[3] Perhaps it is this widely accepted opinion that Samuel Adams was a

---

1. The phrase is from the twentieth century's most comprehensive work on Samuel Adams: John C. Miller, *Sam Adams: Pioneer in Propaganda* (Stanford, 1936).

2. For an excellent survey of the arguments of these historians, see Pauline Maier, *The Old Revolutionaries* (New York, 1980), 6–14.

3. Miller, *Sam Adams*, 227, 228.

shrieker, a mere propagandist who did not mean what he said, that has resulted in so little attention being paid to his arguments.

In her work entitled *The Old Revolutionaries*, Pauline Maier examines carefully the opinion voiced by John C. Miller and others that Samuel Adams was merely an agitator who did not mean what he said. She concludes that Adams' negative reputation is undeserved. Maier argues that Adams was a patient man, possessed of good political sense and slow to advocate violence. The generally accepted opinion of historians is that Adams' hidden purpose from a very early point in the struggle against Great Britain was to bring about a revolution. But Maier finds that Adams did not have an early desire for independence, rather that he decided that independence was the best recourse as late as 1775. Maier's study of his personal and political characteristics leads her to conclude that Samuel Adams is correctly understood according to this model: "Successful revolutionary leaders are not violent and irresponsible anarchists but politic persons of intense discipline for whom the public cause purges mundane considerations of self."[4]

Maier's study of Adams suggests that an examination of his ideas is appropriate, and Adams' importance in bringing about the Revolution suggests that an understanding of his ideas would be critical to an understanding of the political principles of the Revolution. In 1776, sixty-five days before the signing of the Declaration of Independence, Samuel Adams wrote: "We cannot make Events. Our Business is wisely to improve them."[5] Such is what Adams had done successfully for the previous decade and more: he had "improved" events to the point where the Americans were engaged in a war for independence. But what is Adams' standard of wise improvement? There is no single work from Samuel Adams that is as important or as thorough as Dickinson's *Farmer's Letters* or Otis' *Rights of the British Colonies*, but the question can be answered through a careful study of the political arguments Adams made in his many newspaper articles, letters, and papers written for the Massachusetts radicals throughout the revolutionary period.

Adams argued that various acts of the British Parliament from 1764 on violated three sorts of rights belonging to the colonists: their charter rights, their rights as British subjects, and their natural rights as human beings. These three kinds of rights were understood to be

4. Maier, *Old Revolutionaries*, 48, and 3–50 *passim*.
5. *SA*, III, 284.

related, with charter rights and British rights being in the service of the security of natural rights. Those natural rights were understood to include rights to life, liberty, and property.

It was the right to property that was most consistently at issue during the twelve years before the signing of the Declaration of Independence. With the passage of the revenue acts of 1765 and 1767, Adams and the other colonists were faced with taxes imposed by Parliament that they found invaded their right to property.

In 1765 Adams served on a committee appointed by the inhabitants of Boston to draw up instructions for the town's representatives at the General Court. That report begins its criticism of the Stamp Act by pointing out that the act violates the Massachusetts Charter, which gives the power of levying taxes to the Massachusetts General Assembly. Furthermore, the charter grants to the inhabitants of Massachusetts all the rights and privileges of British subjects, including the right to be represented in the body that levies taxes. Since the colonists were not represented in Parliament, then, the Stamp Act violated their rights as British subjects. Those rights of British subjects, the report continues, are based on the "common Rights of Mankind," which include rights to life, liberty, and estate. The arguments made by Adams and his Massachusetts colleagues in 1765 concentrate most on the colonists' right as Britons to be represented in the body that levies taxes. Although they argue that the British constitution has its foundations in the rights of nature, their primary objective is to persuade the Parliament to enforce the right to representation guaranteed by the British constitution.[6]

When the Stamp Act was repealed, it was repealed with an act from Parliament declaring that the colonists had no right to be free from such taxes, indeed from any measures Parliament might choose to pass. Accordingly, the Townshend Acts were passed in 1767, again placing taxes on the colonies. In his argument against these new revenue measures, Adams is more precise and more likely to depend upon natural rights than the rights of British subjects or Massachusetts citizens.

In a 1768 article Adams writes of "the plain and obvious rule of equity whereby the industrious man is intitled to the fruits of his industry." Following John Locke, Adams understands this rule to predate the formation of civil society. "Property is admitted to have an existence in the savage state of nature; and if it is necessary for the

6. See *SA*, I, 9, 17, 29, 30, 38, 45, 54, 64–65.

support of savage life, it by no means becomes less so in civil society." Not only do men have property in the state of nature, but they move out of the state of nature for the clear purpose of securing that property. Government is formed, writes Adams, so that "each individual, under the joint protection of the whole community, may be the Lord of his own possession, and sit securely under his own vine." It follows, then, that "the security of right and property, is the great end of government."[7]

When Adams writes that the purpose of government is to secure people's rights, and especially the right to property, he is making not only a philosophical point but also a descriptive one. That is to say, he understands the British constitution to be designed to secure natural rights: "It is the glory of the British constitution, that it has foundation in the law of God and nature. It is essentially a natural right, that a man shall quietly enjoy, and have the sole disposal of his own property. This right is ingrafted into the British constitution, and is familiar to the American subjects."[8]

The expedient used under the British constitution to maintain the right of each to control his own property is representation. "It is conceived," writes Adams, that the absolute right of each to his own "gave rise in early time to representation in parliament; where every individual in the realm has since been, and is still considered by acts of parliament as present by himself, or by his representative of his own free election."[9] Adams' argument is not that representation is itself a natural right but that it is a constitutional one designed to secure the natural right to property. Representation is the particular fence to private property that the British have chosen to erect. However, the distinction between representation as a natural right and as merely a British right is at times blurred, and Adams never suggests an alternative expedient that governments might use to protect the right to private property.[10] By placing a tax on the colonists, then, Parliament violated both the natural right to property and the right of British subjects to be represented in the taxing body, which latter right was meant to serve the former.

The revenue acts are also understood by Adams to violate charter

7. *SA*, I, 271, 157, 271, 138.
8. *SA*, I, 156–57.
9. *SA*, I, 190.
10. The right to representation appears to be simply a British right in *SA*, I, 29, 30, 38, 45, 171, 190. Adams comes closer to calling representation a natural right in *SA*, I, 64, 172, 180, 288.

rights. In a 1771 article, he uses arguments from Locke to demonstrate that the colonists have no obligation to obey parliamentary legislation, only an obligation to obey the king and the colonial government. According to Locke, writes Adams, a man does not become a perpetual subject merely by living quietly under the laws of a country. "Every man was born naturally free; nothing can make a man a subject of any commonwealth, but his actually entering into it by positive engagement, and express promise & compact." Since there appears to have been no express act of consent to the British government on the colonists' part, when they left Britain to come to America the colonists left behind any obligation to obey the British state. "They were at liberty . . . to incorporate into any other commonwealth, or begin a new one in vacuis locis, in any part of the world they could find free and unpossessed." Out of this freedom, the colonists chose to make a compact with the king of England but not with the whole of the British government. That compact, the Massachusetts Charter, provides that the legislative power—the supreme power of any government—shall consist of the governor, the council, and the house of representatives. "No body can have a power to make laws over a free people, but by their own consent, and by authority received from them: It follows then, either that the people of this province have consented & given authority to the parent state to make laws over them or that she has no such authority."[11]

Nowhere does the charter give any authority to Parliament, and never are the colonists consulted by Parliament in making laws. It follows, then, that the colonists are not bound by the acts of Parliament, "and this is the reason why [the colonists] do not hold themselves rightly oblig'd to submit to the revenue acts now in being."[12]

The charter makes the revenue acts wrong from another perspective. Adams writes that "by our compact with our king . . . we have all the liberties and immunities of Englishmen, to all intents, purposes and constructions whatever; and no King of Great-Britain, were he inclin'd, could have a right either with or without his parliament, to deprive us of those liberties." Those liberties include, as their "principal privilege," Adams writes, "a freedom from all taxes, but such as they shall consent to in person, or by representatives of their

---

11. *SA*, II, 258, 259, 260.

12. *SA*, II, 261. Adams writes that colonists in the past were obliged to obey trade acts from Parliament because they had passed their own laws consenting to do so (*SA*, II, 261).

own free choice and election."[13] The charter, then, guarantees the British right to representation in the taxing body, which right, in turn, is an expedient designed to protect the natural right to private property. The Townshend Acts, like the Stamp Act before them, were argued to violate rights from all three of these interrelated but distinguishable sources. In seeking the security of these rights Adams could urge the king to abide by the charter; he could urge the king and Parliament to be faithful to the British constitution; and he could imply the right to revolt in order to secure the natural right to property.

Samuel Adams' arguments during the Revolution began with a concentration on the right to private property. However, the argument often widened, especially as the years approached 1776, to a more general argument about the right to liberty. Adams' definition of liberty, quoted by him from Montesquieu, is "a Tranquility of Mind arising from the Opinion which each Man has of his own Safety."[14] The safety involved can be physical safety or the safety of the rights of conscience. In the early years of the revolutionary period, however, the thing most considered unsafe was property, so at times it appears that when Adams speaks of the right to liberty he is simply using another way of speaking of the right to property. For example, in a 1772 article Adams quotes John Dickinson in saying that "the parliament's laying taxes on the Colonies for the express purpose of raising a revenue, takes the purse strings out of their hands, and consequently it is 'repugnant to, and subversive of (the end of) our constitution'—Liberty."[15] Yet this statement also indicates the difference between the right to liberty and the right to property. The right to property is violated when property is taken without consent. The right to liberty is violated when a government does something— something like taking the purse strings out of the colonists' hands— that leaves sensible men with the opinion that the right to property may be violated at any future time. The right to property is violated only by an actual taking of property. The right to liberty—as it relates to property—is violated by actions posing the threat that property might be taken away.

Violations of the right to liberty, then, are less obviously oppressive than are violations of the right to property. In the latter case people feel the harm; in the former they must think in order to appre-

13. *SA*, II, 262, I, 140.
14. *SA*, I, 37. See also I, 190, 196, II, 316.
15. *SA*, II, 316.

ciate the danger. During the period after the repeal of most of the Townshend Acts in 1770 and before the passage of the Tea Act in 1773, the political threats to the colonists were threats to liberty and not directly to property. At least partially for that reason, it appears, Adams found it difficult to maintain public concern about the threat from the British government to the colonists' rights. At the end of 1772 Adams found himself hoping for something to "awaken the American Colonies, which have been too long dozing upon the Brink of Ruin."[16]

For, indeed, there were serious violations of the right to liberty that did not bode well for the future of the colonists, as Adams constantly sought to remind his fellow citizens, especially during the quiet period between 1771 and 1773. The sort of danger that became thematic for Adams during that period is indicated by the controversy between Parliament and the New York Assembly over the Mutiny Act. That 1765 act required the colonial assemblies to provide barracks and supplies for British troops quartered in the colonies. The act itself was a threat to property since it was a tax, albeit more indirect than the Stamp Act tax, imposed by Parliament on the colonists. The New York Assembly, which legislated for the colony where the British army in America was headquartered, addressed this unconstitutional tax by refusing to vote the supplies. Parliament's response to New York's act of defiance was to pass a law suspending all acts of the New York Assembly until it should be ready to comply with the Mutiny Act. This suspension indicated Parliament's willingness to attack property both directly, through taxes, and indirectly, through removing the political mechanisms Americans had for providing themselves with some security for their British and natural rights. With regard to Parliament's suspension of the New York Assembly, Adams writes: "A legislative body, without the free exercise of the powers of legislation, is to us incomprehensible. There can be no material difference between such a legislative and none at all."[17]

Parliament's act against the colonial assembly of New York was more dangerous and more obvious a violation of the colonists' liberty than most of the actions taken to change Massachusetts government before the Coercive Acts of 1774. Yet a number of changes, made in the ten years before revolution, had important effects for the colonists' liberty, and Samuel Adams sought constantly to make his fel-

16. *SA*, II, 392.
17. *SA*, I, 147.

low citizens aware of those changes and their implications. One such change had to do with the payment of the salaries of the governor and judges. The governor of Massachusetts was appointed by the Crown, but the colonists had some check over his actions in that his salary came from the colonial assembly. However, at the end of the 1760s it was decided that the governor's salary would come from Britain, and the colonists were left with no lever to make the governor act for the interests of Massachusetts. Adams writes that the payment of the governor by the Crown "under a corrupt administration, it is to be feared, would introduce an absolute government in America; at best it would leave the people in a state of utter uncertainty of their security, which is far from being a state of civil liberty."[18] When Britain created a well-grounded fear of absolute government among the colonists, by Adams' (and Montesquieu's) definition it violated the colonists' right to liberty. Government, according to this definition, need not actually be engaged in tyrannical acts to be tryannical. Tyranny is present when government has the opportunity to act in an arbitrary manner, whether or not it has indeed done so. Adams' forceful rhetoric, especially during the period of the early 1770s, can be neither understood nor appreciated without our keeping in mind these definitions of liberty and tryanny.

In order for the right to liberty to be secure, Adams believes, it is necessary for the people to have some influence in government. "Thanks be to Heaven," he writes in 1768, "the government of Great-Britain has still its proportion of a democracy: The people have their share in the legislature, and no law can be made, nor any publick measures taken, which can affect their interest, without their consent." Adams never presents an alternative to the people's having some voice in government for securing liberty from arbitrary rule. But the king's paying the governor took all real power out of the people's hands, for it left the governor, who had the power to call and prorogue the assembly, free of any effective check by that assembly. The charter, Adams writes, says nothing about who shall pay the governor, but since it is a charter under which the colonists contract for a free government, its purpose demands "that *every* power of it should be properly *controuled* in order to constitute it so." Liberty defined as the people's opinion of their security requires institutional arrangements that protect against arbitrary rule. The right to liberty is infringed when arbitrary rule becomes reasonably possible; it need

18. *SA*, I, 144.

not be actual. That possibility arose in Massachusetts when the governor's salary began to come from the Crown. "But *the people* . . . have understanding enough to know, that a Governor independent of the people for his *support*, as well as his *political Being*, is in fact, a MASTER; and may be, and probably, such is the nature of uncontroulable power, soon will be a TYRANT."[19]

Adams soon found his fears confirmed. The Crown's paying the governor's salary quickly resulted in a government by ministerial instruction. The governor's ruling powers had in effect been assumed by the king's ministers, whose constant instructions to Governor Hutchinson "even annihilate the Powers of the Gov[r] vested in him by the Charter." That is to say, the charter gave the Massachusetts governor the power to act, in certain matters, as he thought necessary for the good of the community. But the absolute instructions from London removed that discretion from the governor and, with it, the possibility of colonial independence from Parliament. Such rule by instruction, according to Adams, violates the charter, the social compact between the people and the king. Adams believes that Governor Hutchinson is a willing participant in this charter violation but argues that even if the Governor had the interest of Massachusetts at heart, it would be impossible for him to pursue that interest with his salary coming from London. Adams sums up his position on the governor in a 1771 letter to Arthur Lee:

> We are in a State of perfect Despotism. Our Governm[t] is essentially alterd. Instead of having a Gov exercising Authority within the Rules & Circumscription of the Charter which is the Compact between the King & the People, & dependent upon the people for his Support, we have a Man with the Name of a Governor only. He is indeed commissioned by the King, but under the Controul of the Minister, to whose Instructions he yields an unlimited Obedience, while he is subsisted with the money of the very people who are thus governd, by virtue of an Assumd Authority of the British Parliament to oblige them to grant him such an annual Stipend as the King shall order.[20]

The same kind of problem—infringement of the right to liberty by removing checks against arbitrary power—arose when, in 1773, it was decided that the justices of the Superior Court in Massachusetts would be paid by the Crown. This measure, Adams argues, removed all independence of the judges and rendered them unable to decide

19. *SA*, I, 273, II, 278, 248.
20. *SA*, II, 67, 173, 342, II, 233.

according to the law rather than according to the wishes of ministers. The people, writes Adams, "clearly saw that this measure would complete the Tragedy of American Freedom, for they could conceive of no state of slavery more perfect, than for Parliament in which they could have no voice to claim a power of making Laws to bind them in all cases whatever, and to exercise that assumed Power in taking their money from them and appropriating it for the support of Judges who are to execute such laws as that parliament should see fit to make binding upon them, and a Fleet and Army to enforce their subjection to them."[21]

Infringements of liberty during the revolutionary decade did not have to do solely with actions that made property unsafe. In addition to the objection the colonists had to supplying the British troops stationed among them, they also objected to the fact that the troops were there. Writing to the governor on behalf of the Massachusetts House of Representatives, Adams states that "the House regard a standing army, posted within the province, in a time of the most profound peace, and uncontroulable by an authority in it, as a dangerous innovation; and a guard of soldiers, with cannon planted at the doors of the State House, while the General Assembly was there held, as the most pointed insult ever offered to a free people, and its whole Legislative."[22]

Adams wrote in an article that the official reason for sending troops to Boston, *i.e.*, that they were needed to control mobs and riots like those in response to the Stamp Act, was not the real reason for the military presence there. Similar riots had occurred elsewhere without British troops being sent in. Therefore, Adams concludes, "It is the part this town has taken on the side of liberty, and its noble exertions in favor of the Rights of America, that render'd it so obnoxious to the tools of power." The Boston Massacre confirmed his fears of the army by showing that the presence of the soldiers indeed made people's rights insecure: "And this military power is allowed to trample upon the laws of the land, the common security, without restraint! Such an instance of absolute uncontroul'd military tyranny must needs be alarming, to those who have before in some measure enjoy'd, and are still entitled to the blessings of a free government."[23] The colonists now believed themselves to be in the position of having their own money wrongfully taken to support troops whose job it was

21. *SA*, III, 85.
22. *SA*, I, 346.
23. *SA*, I, 301, II, 49.

to help enforce laws the colonists were not rightfully obliged to obey. Surely from that perspective the presence of the army was a violation of the right to liberty.

Late in 1772, during the period of relative quiet between the partial repeal of the Townshend Acts and the passing of the Tea Act, when he was trying constantly to maintain his fellow citizens' awareness of the invasion of liberty the British engineered through changes in the colonial government, Samuel Adams made perhaps his most important contribution to bringing about the American Revolution. In a Boston town meeting on November 2, 1772, Adams proposed that a committee be formed to state the beliefs of the people of Boston on the question of their rights and the British violations thereof and to communicate their fears to other towns and to the world. The document the committee produced was entitled "The Rights of the Colonists, a List of Violations of Rights and a Letter of Correspondence." It was circulated; other committees of correspondence were formed; and American fervor in defense of rights was awakened.

Samuel Adams was given the responsibility of drafting the first part of the document, the theoretical statement of the rights of the colonists as men, as Christians, and as British subjects. In his statement he goes to the root of the conflict between the colonists and the mother country. He makes a clear, concise statement of rights that enabled his readers throughout the colonies to appreciate fully the danger of measures like the Crown's payment of gubernatorial and judicial salaries.

Adams begins "The Rights of the Colonists" by discussing the natural rights of human beings, among which are rights to life, liberty, and property, "together with the Right to support and defend them in the best manner they can." These rights are deduced from "the Duty of Self Preservation, commonly called the first Law of Nature."[24] Adams is more sophisticated here in his discussion of natural rights than he had been earlier. Now he states that natural rights carry with them the authority to be defended by the use of whatever means are best suited to the purpose. This assertion implies what he goes on to state, that government in general and the British government in particular are deserving of support only as means to the security of natural rights.

All men may remain in the state of nature as long as they choose. They enter society by consent, forming a compact and agreeing to

24. *SA*, II, 351.

give up certain rights, *i.e.*, only those that impinge upon the good of the whole, but maintaining every natural right not expressly ceded. By entering into society, a man chooses to give up the right to be sole judge of his rights and of injuries done to them, and agrees to "an Arbiter or indifferent Judge between him and his neighbours," which arbiter he should, of course, pay. "In short," Adams concludes the section on natural rights, "it is the greatest absurdity to suppose it in the power of one or any number of men at the entering into society, to renounce their essential natural rights, or the means of preserving those rights when the great end of civil government from the very nature of its institution is for the support, protection, and defense of those very rights."[25]

In the section on natural rights, Adams writes that religious toleration is "in the fullest extent consistent with the being of civil society."[26] In context, this conclusion must follow from the argument that human beings' natural liberty is constrained upon their entering society only to the extent necessary to reach the end of society, which is to secure natural rights. In general, regulation of religion seems unnecessary to meet this goal. There are, however, exceptions in the cases of religious doctrines that pose a threat to civil society, and religions that preach such doctrines must not be tolerated. For this reason, writes Adams, Roman Catholics should not be tolerated because their doctrines place a human power, the pope, above the civil power and may serve to create anarchy and confusion, leaving life, liberty, and property insecure. This conclusion about general religious tolerance from the argument about natural rights is reinforced in the short section on "the Rights of the Colonists as Christians." There Adams argues that religious toleration, except of Papists, is provided for by act of Parliament and by the colonial charters.

The third section of Adams' statement is on "the Rights of the Colonists as Subjects." In this section Adams argues that all British subjects have a right to a government that seeks to secure personal security, personal liberty, and private property.[27] Therefore they have a right to a nonarbitrary legislative power as well as to representation in any body that acts to take their property from them. These rights are supported by colonial charter but, more important, by acts of the British Parliament.

There is nothing in "The Rights of the Colonists" that does not

25. *SA*, II, 353, 354.
26. *SA*, II, 352.
27. *SA*, II, 356.

appear, though perhaps with less clarity, earlier in Adams' writings. What makes the document noteworthy is its strong concentration on natural rights as the ground for the colonists' dispute with Great Britain. As presented in "The Rights of the Colonists," the fundamental issues are not interpretations of the British constitution or of colonial charters. The concentration on natural rights now makes those issues relatively unimportant. The issues are life, liberty, and property; and the strong, clear argument about natural rights Adams presents makes it plain that whatever the status of various legal conventions, those rights are justly defended by the colonists. This is a critical change in emphasis from the period of the Stamp Act crisis, when the concentration of Adams' arguments was on British and charter rights, and only through them on natural rights.

According to at least one observer, in "The Rights of the Colonists" Samuel Adams presented the teaching on the natural rights of the colonists more clearly than anyone had yet done. The document was widely published, both in the colonies and in England, and it helped to solidify opinion both for and against the American cause. Adams, who was not given to celebrating his own importance, allowed that "perhaps no measure that has been taken by the Town of Boston during our present Struggles for Liberty, has thwarted the designs of our enemies more" than the acceptance and dissemination of "The Rights of the Colonists."[28]

Adams does not mention a right to revolution in "The Rights of the Colonists," but that is merely because he does not explicitly draw the logical conclusion of his argument. From the time of the Stamp Act crisis on, Adams' arguments imply a right to revolution, the implication becoming stronger as the arguments center more on natural rights and less on the rights of British subjects.

It is not at all surprising that Adams always implies the right to revolution when one realizes that his arguments about natural rights and the role of government in securing them come almost always from John Locke. It would be difficult to overestimate the importance of "the immortal Locke" for Adams' thought and writing. Other political philosophers are mentioned—Emmerich de Vattel occasionally in a supportive role, Montesquieu on the definition of liberty and the purpose of the British constitution, and Richard Hooker from passages quoted in Locke—but Locke has the leading role. His writ-

28. Philip Davidson, *Propaganda and the American Revolution* (Chapel Hill, 1941), 112; *SA*, III, 28.

ings are used to provide major themes and arguments at critical points. At one place Adams writes: "Mr. Locke has often been quoted in the present dispute between Britain and her colonies, and very much to our purpose. His reasoning is so forcible, that no one has even attempted to confute it." Thus Adams quotes Locke's *Second Treatise of Civil Government* in arguing that the purpose of government is to secure property; he quotes him extensively in arguing that property may not be taken without consent; he uses Locke's argument to conclude that express consent is necessary to bind a man to a civil society; and he quotes Locke's argument that legislatures may not assume arbitrary power.[29] Adams quotes Locke four times in "The Rights of the Colonists."

Of course, Locke suggests that the people may revolt when government fails to meet its end. In 1770 Adams quietly refers to the right to revolution in a long quotation on prerogative from Locke's *Second Treatise:* "Between an executive Power in being with such a Prerogative, and a Legislative that depends upon his Will for their convening, there can be no Judge on Earth, as there can be none between the Legislative & the People, should either the Executive or Legislative when they have got the Power in their Hands, design or go about to enslave or destroy them. The People have no other Remedy in this, as in all other Cases, where they have no Judge on Earth, but to appeal to Heaven."[30]

By 1773 Adams had begun to blame the king for failing to protect the colonists against parliamentary usurpations. The king, then, was not only failing to secure property, in violation of the compact between king and colonists, but also cooperating in violations of the colonists' rights to property and liberty. "The people," writes Adams in 1775, "hold the Invasion of their Rights & Liberties the most horrid rebellion and a Neglect to defend them against any Power whatsoever the highest Treason." In this he follows Locke's argument that when the government takes away rather than secures the people's property, it has rebelled and the people must defend themselves. By 1775 Adams had given up on the rights of British subjects: any government that could become as arbitrary as the British government had become in the previous ten years could not be a dependable guard over the

29. *SA*, II, 326, 298–99, 316, 210, 200, 257.
30. *SA*, II, 22. The quotation is from Locke's *Second Treatise*, sec. 168. On the connection between an "appeal to heaven" and the use of force in Locke, see *Second Treatise*, sec. 21.

people's rights.[31] Now the only important argument was about natural rights, and Locke's argument led inescapably to the conclusion that the colonies must rebel to secure those rights.

In the period leading to the Revolutionary War, Samuel Adams' political writings were clearly and consistently informed by the political philosophy of John Locke. Of the major figures of the American Revolution, no other seems to have followed Locke more thoroughly than Adams. But in 1775, with the Revolution underway, Adams' writings began to concentrate upon a new theme. Like his fellow American politicians, he was required to turn his thoughts from the destruction of governments to their creation. Now that Americans were ridding themselves of the tyrannical British government, they could have governments that could do what governments ought to do—produce virtue in the citizens. "I hope," Adams wrote to Elbridge Gerry in 1775, "you will improve the golden opportunity of restoring the ancient purity of principles and manners in our county." Two months later, in a letter to James Warren, he expressed his continued concern about the degeneration of morals: "Certainly the People do not already hanker after the Onions & the Garlick!" It was Adams who, in 1780, made mention of his desire to see Boston as "the *Christian* Sparta."[32]

Adams' concern for using the power of the state to produce virtue might appear to create a certain confusion about the goal of the American Revolution. He now seems to desire to establish the good society of classical political thought rather than a civil society whose purpose is to secure individual rights. Inspection of Adams' arguments, however, leads to the conclusion that his political concern for virtue, although genuine, was secondary rather than primary, that his opinion remained that governments exist to secure human beings' natural rights to life, liberty, and property.

The context of the letter within which Adams speaks of "the *Christian* Sparta" clarifies his priorities: "I once thought, that City would be the *Christian* Sparta. But Alas! Will men never be free! They will be free no longer than while they remain virtuous." The virtues of a Sparta here appear desirable because they contribute to the maintenance of freedom. This connection between virtue and liberty is made clear in a 1775 letter to James Warren. Adams makes a distinc-

31. *SA*, III, 57, 197, 262.
32. *SA*, III, 231, 244, IV, 238.

tion between political virtues and vices and private virtues and vices. The political ones—corruption, dishonesty, extravagance—when owned by rulers tend to be the destruction of states. If the people's liberties are to be preserved, these vices must be avoided. However, there is a strong connection between public and private virtues and vices: "There is seldom an Instance of a Man guilty of betraying his Country, who had not before lost the Feeling of moral Obligations in his private Connections."[33] Therefore it is necessary to use the power of government to encourage the formation of virtue of all sorts so as to maintain political virtue and government dedicated to the security of individual rights.

Similar reasoning applies to the voters. They must be educated to virtue so that they will use their votes well. "Thus far as [elected officials] are accountable to the people, as they are lyable for Misbehavior to be discarded; but this is not a sufficient Security to the People unless they are themselves *virtuous*." Adams' dedication to virtue as a goal of public policy is based upon the calculation that "after all, virtue is the surest means of securing the public liberty."[34] Virtue is seen by Adams as a means to the security of life, liberty, and property.

In looking to virtue to provide justice and stability in American politics, Adams is following the conventional wisdom that republics can work only with a virtuous citizenry. Still, it is perhaps a weakness in Adams' thought that he does not appreciate the difficulty of what he expects: a regime whose goal is the security of individual rights producing in its citizens real selfless virtue. Sparta, after all, was not dedicated to the pursuit of private fortunes. Yet the fact that Samuel Adams does not have the subtlety of *The Federalist* to realize what means must be employed to secure individual rights does not change the more important fact that as a political man Samuel Adams always aimed his labors at creating a government for Americans that would secure their natural rights.

"Perhaps," Adams writes in a 1771 article, "there was never a people who discovered themselves more strongly attached to their natural and constitutional rights and liberties, than the British Colonists on this American Continent."[35] Samuel Adams' rhetoric is designed to remind his fellow citizens of that attachment and to educate them as to the dangers presented to their liberties by British

33. *SA*, IV, 238, III, 236.
34. *SA*, III, 245, 231.
35. *SA*, II, 204–205.

policies. His political thought is not original, but his application of principles to the American situation is based upon a careful understanding of both principles and circumstances, and his resulting arguments are forceful, clear, and consistent. It is not enough to say that Samuel Adams incited revolution; it must be added that he incited revolution by arguing vigorously that revolution was the just choice for Americans to make.

FIVE

John Adams

❦

John Adams is a most important figure in American revolutionary thought and politics. General commentators on the thought of the Revolution tend to depend upon Adams more than any other author as a source for explaining what the Revolution was all about.[1] One reason for this dependence is that Adams was very influential in Boston radical politics, in colonial revolutionary politics as a leading member of the Continental Congress, and in the creation of the new governments that came with the Revolution. The special attention given to Adams by students of eighteenth-century American political thought, however, does not stem merely from the fact that he was one of the country's most influential politicians. It stems from the fact that he was the most thoughtful of those influential revolutionary politicians. Gordon Wood observes that "no one read more and thought more about law and politics" during the revolutionary period than Adams. Pauline Maier adds that Adams was "perhaps the country's most learned student of politics."[2]

Like his cousin Samuel, John Adams was active throughout the revolutionary period. The discussion in this chapter, therefore, will include various materials from the entire period. But the analysis of Adams will concentrate on the writing in which he presents his most complete, thorough, and famous presentation of the colonists' case

1. See, for example, Gordon S. Wood, *The Creation of the American Republic, 1776–1787* (Chapel Hill, 1969), and Bernard Bailyn, *The Ideological Origins of the American Revolution* (Cambridge, 1967). Adams receives the longest entry of the American revolutionaries in the indexes of both works.

2. Wood, *Creation of the American Republic*, 568; Pauline Maier, *From Resistance to Revolution* (New York, 1972), 287.

against Great Britain, the letters he published under the pseudonym "Novanglus" in 1774 and 1775. The consideration of the issues from Adams' writings—from the charges he levels against the British and British officials in Massachusetts to his understanding of the goals of politics and of the British threat to the secure achievement of those goals, to Adams' understanding of the limits on the ability of political action to achieve perfection—should lead us to appreciate the fact that John Adams' political thought and action during the revolutionary period were indeed based upon a careful and complex understanding of politics.

There is much discussion in the writings of John Adams from the period preceding revolution about a conspiracy against the liberties of the colonists. This is especially the case in the "Novanglus" letters. There he writes frequently of a "junto" whose members had conspired to deny the colonists their rights. Adams began "Novanglus" with an intent to "show the wicked policy of the tories; trace their plan from its first rude sketches to its present complete draught; show that it has been much longer in contemplation than is generally known."[3] There was, to his mind, a considerable amount of evidence to prove the existence of the conspiracy, and he proceeds in "Novanglus" to develop that evidence.

The first member of the "junto" he undertakes to discuss is Francis Bernard, Governor of Massachusetts during the 1760s. In 1764 Bernard had offered to the British ministry a pamphlet entitled "Principles of Law and Polity," in which he advocated a new modeling of American governments. The pamphlet was written during the Stamp Act crisis, and it is Adams' contention that the proposals Bernard makes therein were designed to create an effective system for taxing the colonists without their consent. The pamphlet includes an assertion of the absolute right of Parliament to legislate for the colonies. It later recommends alterations on American governments, including the recision of colonial charters, the establishment of a nobility appointed by the king for life (ultimately to be hereditary), and the redrawing of colonial boundaries.[4] Once these proposals are known, Adams argues, nothing more is necessary for him to prove Bernard's hostility to American liberties.

Having exposed Bernard's opinions, Adams turns to another member of this "junto," Bernard's successor as governor, Thomas

3. *JA*, IV, 13.
4. *JA*, IV, 25–28.

Hutchinson. Adams considered Hutchinson to be the greatest threat to American liberties. The evidence of the danger Hutchinson posed to the colonists' liberties came basically from two sources. The first had to do with separation of powers, an expedient for which Hutchinson appeared to have little concern. In 1765 he was lieutenant governor, chief justice, judge of a probate court, and a member of the council. That is, he held high office in the legislative branch, the second highest office in the executive branch, and the highest office in the judicial branch. To the colonists this dangerous concentration of power in the hands of one man appeared to continue when Hutchinson became governor, for at that time the offices of lieutenant governor and chief justice, which he gave up on becoming governor, were filled by his in-laws, Andrew and Peter Oliver.

The second, and more serious, kind of evidence to support the charge that Hutchinson was the greatest danger to colonial liberty came from an analysis of his policies. In "Novanglus," Adams registers his agreement "that it was not the persons of Bernard, Hutchinson, or Oliver, that made them obnoxious; but their principles and practices." Despite the fact that Hutchinson thought it impolitic on the part of the British government to lay taxes on the Americans, he defended consistently, frequently, and publicly Parliament's absolute right to legislate in all cases for the colonies. In "Novanglus," Adams seeks to explain how Hutchinson had become more and more hated in Massachusetts. He lost many friends, Adams suggests, when "in one of his first speeches [as governor] he took care to advance the supreme authority of parliament."⁵

For Adams, as for the other revolutionaries, the single most important piece of evidence of Hutchinson's complicity in a conspiracy to restrict American liberties came through Benjamin Franklin. In 1773 Franklin sent some letters Hutchinson and others had written to British correspondents to Boston, where they were published. In one of Hutchinson's letters there was the fatal statement that "there must be an abridgment of what are called English liberties" in the colonies. For those who had been paying attention to Hutchinson over the years, the statement was neither new nor surprising; it was, for Hutchinson, a simple conclusion that followed from the fact that the supreme governing authority for the American colonies was an ocean away. To the revolutionaries the statement seemed clear and

5. *JA*, IV, 66–67, 70; Bernard Bailyn, *The Ordeal of Thomas Hutchinson* (Cambridge, 1974), 297.

irrefutable evidence that the man in Massachusetts who was most listened to by the British ministry and who had the most governmental power thought it necessary to restrict the liberties of the colonists. Hutchinson's letter made him the most visible and dangerous enemy to American liberties in Massachusetts.

The revolutionary struggle was over liberty. On the one hand was Adams' perception that liberty was seriously endangered; on the other was Hutchinson's argument that there was no serious threat and that those who thought there was were moved by irrational fears. One cannot appreciate Adams' position without understanding what he believed liberty to be and why he thought it so valuable.

There is in John Adams' work, as there is in the work of most of the revolutionary statesmen, little space spent defining terms. Since the object of their writing was most often immediately political rather than speculative, the revolutionaries did not need to discuss the meaning of terms their readers easily understood. Apparently liberty was such a term. Perhaps the most instructive source in Adams' writing on the meaning and importance of liberty is his 1765 "Dissertation on the Canon and Feudal Law."

Adams writes that the history of human society demonstrates that the great have always attempted to prevent the people from learning of their rights. "I say RIGHTS, for such they have, undoubtedly, antecedent to all earthly government,—*Rights* that cannot be repealed or restrained by human laws—*Rights*, derived from the great Legislator of the universe." Since the establishment of Christianity, he continues, the two most effective systems employed by the great to prevent the people from knowing and defending their rights are the canon law and the feudal law. The Roman clergy were able to satisfy their desire for power by keeping people in a state of ignorance through teaching them that the clergy controlled not only the eternal salvation of human beings but also natural events on the earth. The feudal law began "for the necessary defence of a barbarous people" but soon was adopted by most princes of Europe due to their "tyranny, cruelty, and lust." In Europe the two systems of tyranny combined to support one another, and "as long as this confederacy lasted, and the people were held in ignorance, liberty, and with her, knowledge and virtue too, seem to have deserted the earth, and one age of darkness succeeded another."[6]

With the Reformation, Adams writes, the chains were broken and

6. *JA*, III, 449, 450, 451.

people began to understand their rights. With this understanding there grew a struggle between the people and the temporal and spiritual tyrants, which struggle resulted in the settlement of America. "It was not religion alone, as is commonly supposed; but it was a love of universal liberty, and a hatred, a dread, a horror, of the infernal confederacy before described, that projected, conducted, and accomplished the settlement of America." The American settlers chose to abandon the tyranny of Europe in order to secure liberty. In establishing systems of government with this goal in mind, Adams tells us, the Americans were seeking government "more agreeable to the dignity of human nature, than any they had seen in Europe."[7]

Liberty, then, appears to be this much: it is the opposite of absolute arbitrary rule; it is self-control; it is the freedom for self-development. This is not to say that liberty requires anarchy. Adams argues that government is a necessary result of the fact that man is a social animal. Instinct causes man to form society, and government is needed to regulate society for the happiness of its members. Indeed, Adams denies that liberty is inconsistent with monarchy. Liberty, however, requires rational rule, so it is inconsistent with government by fear and superstition. Liberty is something human beings possess as a matter of right but not, it seems, something human beings always or even usually possess in actuality. For although there is in human nature "a veneration for liberty," according to Adams, it is possible to stifle this natural love in human beings by treating them in subhuman ways.[8]

There is, for Adams, a strong relationship between the natural desire for liberty and the human capacity for intellectual improvement. "And liberty," he writes, "cannot be preserved without a general knowledge among the people, who have a right, from the frame of their nature, to knowledge, as their great Creator, who does nothing in vain, has given them understandings, and a desire to know." The desire for liberty is stifled only by rulers who take care to keep their subjects ignorant. As subjects become more human—that is, as the distinctively human capacity of reason is developed—men understand their right to control themselves with that reason and seek, as human beings, to exercise that right. Thus is it that "an enemy to liberty" is "an enemy to human nature."[9]

7. *JA*, III, 451, 453.
8. L. H. Butterfield (ed.), *Diary and Autobiography of John Adams* (4 vols.; Cambridge, 1963), II, 57; *JA*, III, 452, IV, 14.
9. *JA*, III, 456, 470.

The Americans, writes Adams, "have the most habitual and radical sense of liberty." It was for liberty that they came to America, and once here they have taken care to maintain an educated populace that is required to understand the value of liberty. Moreover, according to Adams in 1765, they believe they exist under a government whose purpose is to supply liberty, that government being government under the British constitution. A constitution, Adams writes, is a "combination of powers for a certain end, namely,—the good of the whole community." The distinctive feature of the British constitution is the Britons' understanding that "liberty is essential to the public good," a realization that leads to this fact about the British constitution: "Liberty is its end, its use, its designation, drift, and scope." Adams argues that in order to achieve its goal of liberty the British constitution employs the expedient of giving the people a share of both the legislative and the executive powers. The people's share of the latter is to be found in the jury system, and they share in the former in that laws cannot be made without the consent of a popularly elected branch of the legislature. In an essay published in 1766, there are passages in which Adams discusses these two popular powers and communicates clearly both his feeling for liberty and his understanding of its necessity for human beings:

> What a fine reflection and consolation it is for a man, that he can be subjected to no laws which he does not make himself, or constitute some of his friends to make for him. . . . What a satisfaction it is to reflect, that he can lie under the imputation of no guilt, be subjected to no punishment . . . but by the judgment of his peers, his equals, his neighbors.

> In these two powers consist wholly the liberty and security of the people. They have no other fortification against wanton, cruel power; no other indemnification against being ridden like horses, fleeced like sheep, worked like cattle, and fed and clothed like swine and hounds; no other defence against fines, imprisonments, whipping-posts, gibbets, bastinadoes, and racks.[10]

John Adams understood the purpose of British rule to be liberty, the right of individuals to develop themselves free from absolute, arbitrary government. The American colonists believed that in order to secure this liberty the British constitution provided for certain means of government and limits on government that would prevent government from becoming arbitrary and absolute. During the revo-

10. *JA*, III, 475, 479, 482–83.

lutionary period Adams and his colleagues argued that these means of government were being changed and the limits violated. Adams' arguments on these points tend to be legalistic and often tedious, but they are the arguments on which his revolutionary activity depended.

The most frequently discussed issue of the revolutionary period was, of course, the issue of taxation. Adams argues in "Novanglus" that the primary objective of the "junto" was to obtain a revenue from the colonists through acts of Parliament. According to the colonists, with each of the taxing measures—the Stamp Act, the Townshend Acts, and the Tea Act—Parliament was violating a fundamental principle of British liberty designed to protect the people from absolute power. "We have always understood it to be a grand and fundamental principle of the constitution," writes Adams for the town of Braintree in 1765, "that no freeman should be subject to any tax to which he has not given his own consent, in person or by proxy."[11] Since the colonists had no representation in Parliament, it was a violation of their liberty for Parliament to tax them.

His point about taxation was the single most important one for Adams during the revolutionary period, but it was also part of a larger argument: that without the colonists' consent, Parliament has no authority whatever to legislate for them. In "Novanglus" Adams makes this argument by analyzing the origins of the colonies. Once the original colonists left England with the king's permission, he argues, they became natural free agents, with the exception that they did maintain their allegiance to the king and would have been required to return to England had the king so ordered. But in the new land, and outside the English nation, they were not bound by the laws of England and had a natural right to create their own government. They were "entitled to the common law of England when they emigrated, that is, to just so much of it as they pleased to adopt, and no more." They had "a clear right to have erected in this wilderness a British constitution, or a perfect democracy, or any other form of government they saw fit."[12]

Now the particular political arrangement the emigrants chose to establish maintained their allegiance to the king but did not make them subject to Parliament. They made a contract with the king to

11. *JA*, IV, 23, III, 466.
12. *JA*, IV, 122.

exchange allegiance (which the original settlers still owed to the king, but which their posterity did not) for protection. They did not thereby make the king absolute, for their charters, which were the contracts, required the king to protect the liberties of Englishmen. The critical point is that the contracts were only with the king, not with the realm and not with Parliament. Adams takes a great deal of space in "Novanglus" to argue the legality and propriety of this system whereby the Americans would owe obedience to the king but not to Parliament. He presents a detailed discussion of the relationships between the king, Parliament, and other English possessions, including Wales, Ireland, Jersey, and Guernsey. In addition, he discusses legal precedents involving actions of the king and actions of colonial assemblies to show that, though there are a very few statements to the contrary, "the authority of parliament was never generally acknowledged in America."[13] The conclusion Adams draws from argument and legal evidence is that Parliament has no authority to legislate for the American colonies.

Yet some parliamentary authority—the authority to regulate trade—has always been recognized by Americans. Adams argues, however, that this authority, though real and generally acknowledged, does not refute the argument that in contracting with the king the Americans did not accept rule by Parliament. Parliament's authority to regulate trade is part of a separate transaction whereby the colonists, sensitive to the advantages of a uniform trade policy for the king's dominions, contracted to give Parliament the authority to regulate trade, but only that specific authority. Adams writes: "The whigs allow that, from the necessity of a case not provided for by common law . . . America has all along consented, still consents, and ever will consent, that parliament, being the most powerful legislature in the dominions, should regulate the trade of the dominions. This is founding the authority of parliament to regulate our trade, upon *compact* and *consent* of the colonies." As evidence of this compact, he points to a 1677 Massachusetts statute expressing such an agreement.[14] Adams' argument, then, is that Parliament has authority to regulate trade, but that any attempt to raise a revenue through imposing taxes is a violation of the liberty—guaranteed to them by contract with the king—to be represented in the body making laws

13. *JA*, IV, 126, 47.
14. *JA*, IV, 99–100, 111–12.

for them. Parliament's repeated attempts to tax the colonists are to Adams attempts to deny the colonists their liberty through the imposition of an unjust, illegal, and arbitrary governing power.

Parliament's laying of taxes upon the colonists and, more important, the king's support of Parliament's claim to the absolute authority to do so posed a double threat to the Americans' liberties. In removing the colonists' property without their consent, the revenue acts directly violated their liberty. In asserting the absolute right to legislate for the colonies in all cases, Parliament assaulted the colonists' liberties more indirectly by threatening that it might act at any time to violate the rights of Englishmen. There was plenty of evidence for Adams during the revolutionary period that the British government had no qualms about violating those rights, especially if such violations would help to enforce the revenue acts.

Adams believed that the first evidence of the British government's willingness to violate colonial rights had come before the revenue acts. In a letter he wrote to Abigail on July 3, 1776, in which he celebrated the culmination of the contest between the colonies and Britain, Adams placed the beginning of the controversy not in 1765 with the Stamp Act but in 1761.[15] In that year a parliamentary act allowing customs officials to be granted writs of assistance (general search warrants) began to be used in the colonies. Whig lawyers challenged the constitutionality of the writs, arguing that they violated the colonists' fundamental rights. Then Chief Justice Hutchinson found in favor of the government for the simple and clear reason that the writs were legal according to parliamentary statute. That decision posed the issue that was to become much more important in future years: Parliament's raw power to pass laws was pitted against the Americans' liberty.

In the "Instructions of the Town of Boston To Their Representatives," written in 1769, John Adams states that "next to the revenue itself, the late extensions of the jurisdiction of the admiralty are our greatest grievance." The admiralty courts had always had jurisdiction over trade matters, but before the 1760s the colonists had managed to keep the courts' importance in American life minimal. In the 1760s, their jurisdiction over trade and navigation began to be enforced. What was still more threatening, however, was that in addition to their normal jurisdiction, the admiralty courts were given jurisdic-

15. L. H. Butterfield (ed.), *Adams Family Correspondence* (2 vols.; Cambridge, 1963), II, 28.

tion over cases arising under the Stamp Act and other new measures of the 1760s. Adams explains the threat to liberty in this passage: "In these courts one judge presides alone! No juries have any concern there! The law and fact are both to be decided by the same single judge, whose commission is only during pleasure."[16] These were precisely the attributes of the admiralty courts that Parliament wanted to use. It was Parliament's judgment that colonial juries could not be trusted to enforce the revenue measures, so it took the power of judicial enforcement away from juries and gave it to judges who held their positions solely at the king's pleasure. For Adams, this act constituted a most serious threat, for it removed one of the two most important institutions designed to preserve liberty and maintain the dignity of the people. The curtailment of the power of juries was a dangerous event, especially when its purpose was to further the important denial of liberty contained in the revenue acts.

The other major issue that Adams and his fellow revolutionaries saw as a severe threat to liberty was the Crown's paying the salaries of the governor and judges. Until the revolutionary period the colonial legislatures had been responsible for paying the Crown-appointed executive and judicial officials. It was an arrangement the colonists valued highly, for it was the only method they had to check these officials in order to ensure some faithfulness to the needs and desires of the people. When the people's opinions began to conflict sharply with those of the British government, however, that government sought to strengthen its ability to impose its will on the colonies and to weaken the colonists' power to resist. The measure made the judges and the governor simply British officials rather than colonial ones.

One indication of the importance of this issue to Adams is the fact that he wrote a lengthy series of articles on the subject of the independence of the judiciary. His opponent in argument, William Brattle, argued that Adams and his fellows should be happy to have the judges' salaries paid by the Crown, for that would lift a burden from the colonists' pocketbooks but not threaten liberty because judges served during good behavior. Adams responded that he would have agreed with Brattle had it been true that colonial judges served during good behavior—that is, as long as they chose to serve unless they committed an impeachable offense—and therefore could be expected to resist pressure to violate the law at the desire of the ministry.

16. *JA*, III, 507, 466.

However, Adams argued, such was not the case. He presented a long, detailed, learned legal argument to prove what was in fact the case, that colonial judges served during pleasure. In "Novanglus" Adams summarizes the Americans' position on the salaries issue with these words: "They uniformly think that the destruction of their charter, making the council and judges wholly dependent upon the crown, and the people subjected to the unlimited power of parliament as their supreme legislative, is slavery."[17]

The most disturbing acts of the British in the revolutionary period were attempts to impose the absolute power of Parliament upon the colonists. The reason for these unconstitutional, unjust impositions of arbitrary power, it seemed to Adams, was Parliament's desire to obtain a revenue from the colonists. In addition, the British used soldiers in order to quell resistance to the acts. On this point, Adams later makes this recollection: "Their very Appearance in Boston was a strong proof to me, that the determination in Great Britain to subjugate Us, was too deep and inveterate to be altered by Us."[18] To Adams, then, government action piled upon government action to show clearly a design—a conspiracy—to remove the colonists' ability to govern themselves and to place over them absolute and arbitrary rule.

Adams saw the violations of colonial rights that began with the writs of assistance in 1761 and continued for the next fifteen years as serious indeed. But far more serious to him was the principle that lay behind the acts of the British government during the period—the principle of absolute parliamentary control over the colonies. Were this principle to become solidly established through colonial acquiescence in its implementation, Adams feared that future parliamentary actions could prove far more devastating to the Americans than anything done in the period from 1761 through 1776.

Adams argues, then, that it is of the utmost importance for the Americans to refuse to allow the principle of parliamentary supremacy over the colonists to become well established. Quoting Tacitus, he notes that "the first advances of tyranny are steep and perilous, but, when once you are entered, parties and instruments are ready to espouse you." It is essential, then, to "nip the shoots of arbitrary power in the bud." Such is not an easy task because citizens tend to take liberties for granted. Moreover, even when a threat to liberty is identified, it requires immediate sacrifice on the people's

17. *JA*, III, 511–74, IV, 54.
18. Butterfield (ed.), *Diary and Autobiography*, III, 290.

part to still the threat. In the short run the more comfortable path for people to follow is to appease the tyranny in its early stages when it is merely laying the foundation for future power. A people who would keep its liberty must understand the danger of such appeasement and must be willing to sacrifice for its long-term interest. The great danger Adams feared was that at some point the Americans would take the easy way of submitting to a parliamentary tax, thereby admitting Parliament's authority to tax them. Yet the Americans did not seem to succumb to the temptation to sacrifice future liberty for present comfort. Adams writes of them in 1765: "They have a pious Horror of consenting to any Thing, which may intail slavery on their Posterity. They think that the Liberties of Mankind and the Glory of human Nature is in their Keeping."[19]

By 1773 Adams was not so confident of his countrymen's ability to appreciate and act against dangerous parliamentary actions. The Tea Act of that year was, to him, the most threatening act yet. In 1770, in response to colonial pressure, Parliament had repealed all of the duties established by the Townshend Acts except the one on tea. Following that, Parliament passed legislation in 1773 changing the rules affecting the operation of the East India Company in such a way that, despite the tax, tea would become actually less expensive in the colonies.

Adams feared that the lower price on tea would tempt his fellow citizens to ignore principle and acquiesce in parliamentary taxation. Here the danger of "ignorance, inattention, and disunion," through which nearly "all Mankind have lost their liberties" was great. But Adams was heartened by the Americans' response to the temptation to ignore the principle of parliamentary taxation when, on December 16, 1773, a group of Bostonians threw a cargo of tea into the harbor to keep it from being unloaded and sold in the colonies. The Boston Tea Party, Adams says, was an "absolute necessity" to prevent those who were supporting the nascent despotism from succeeding, but not only the Tories: "To this tribe of the *wicked* . . . must be added another, perhaps more numerous, of the *weak*; who never could be brought to think of the consequences of their actions, but would gratify their appetites if they could come at the means." These weak could not be counted on to consider posterity in the face of cheap tea. Adams writes that those who participated in the Tea Party and refused to repent "saw the ruin of their country connected with such a com-

19. *JA*, III, 490, IV, 43; Butterfield (ed.), *Diary and Autobiography*, I, 282.

pliance, and their own involved in it. . . . Several of them could have paid for the tea and never have felt the loss. They knew they must suffer vastly more than the tea was worth; but they thought they acted for America and posterity."[20]

Adams' support for the Boston Tea Party, however, should not be taken as evidence that he was unconcerned about the danger involved in using violent or illegal means to redress colonial grievances. He was by nature politically conservative. His public and private writings betray that conservatism both before and after the Revolution. He is acutely aware of the danger of a spirit of anarchy involved in the struggle against the British. Time and time again Adams writes of the evils of irrational mobs, of the danger that they would attack all order. He knows that mob violence is a tool to be used only rarely and with great caution. In the "Dissertation on the Canon and the Feudal Law," Adams writes of the spirit of liberty that "this spirit, however, without knowledge, would be little better than a brutal rage." His political goal is not simple liberty but *ordered* liberty, and so he encourages that "all become attentive to the grounds and principles of government." Elsewhere, Adams gives this caution to his countrymen: "Let us not be bubbled then out of our reverence and obedience to government, on the one hand; nor out of our right to think and act for ourselves in our own department on the other." He continues on to say that "it becomes necessary to every subject, then, to be in some degree a statesman, and to examine and judge for himself of the tendency of political principles and measures."[21]

In "Novanglus" Adams quotes with approval John Locke's argument that the people are slow to revolt and will suffer many evils before undertaking the extreme measure of revolt. For Adams this is as it should be. He feels "a strong aversion to . . . partial and irregular Recurrences to original Power." Such recurrences are to be justified by this calculus: "Every principle of reason, justice, and prudence, in such cases, demands that the least mischief shall be done, the least evil, among a number shall always be preferred." In 1774 he writes to Abigail that "if Popular Commotions can be justifyed, in Opposition to Attacks upon the Constitution, it can only be when Fundamentals are invaded, nor then unless for absolute Necessity and with great Caution."[22]

20. *JA*, IV, 94, 90, 93.

21. Butterfield (ed.), *Diary and Autobiography*, I, 260, III, 290, 298–99, 326; Butterfield (ed.), *Adams Family Correspondence*, I, 124–25, 126, 131; *JA*, III, 462, 437.

22. *JA*, IV, 89; Butterfield (ed.), *Adams Family Correspondence*, III, 299, I, 131.

In his attempts to balance the evil of mob violence with the evil of despotism, Adams ultimately makes his decision on the basis of the importance of liberty to human beings and of the seriousness of the threat to liberty presented by the principle of absolute parliamentary authority. He concludes that to allow a right so valuable to human beings to be removed without a fight is a greater evil than to fight. He says that in such a fight the people, even if they lose, cannot be unsuccessful: "because, if they live, they can be but slaves, after an unfortunate effort, and slaves they would have been, if they had not resisted. So that nothing is lost. If they die, they cannot be said to lose, for death is better than slavery. If they succeed their gains are immense. They preserve their liberties."[23]

23. *JA*, IV, 17.

Thomas Jefferson

Among the names of the American revolutionary thinkers, Thomas Jefferson's name is the one best known. His just renown as a revolutionary derives largely from his authorship of the Declaration of Independence. That authorship makes him a man whose thought it is essential to understand in order to understand the political thought of the American Revolution. Jefferson's involvement in the crisis began fairly late, with his first major intellectual contribution coming in 1774. He did not share in the task of educating the colonists in the political theory that led to the Revolution for as long as Otis, Henry, the Adamses, and Dickinson did. Still, his importance for the revolutionary generation is immense, and his importance for succeeding generations can hardly be overstated. He authored the declaration that spelled out clearly and forcefully the principles that united the colonists in revolution, and he thus reinforced those principles among the revolutionaries and explained them to Americans ever since.

Jefferson's first major political writing was a proposed set of instructions for the Virginia delegates to the Continental Congress in 1774, later published as a pamphlet entitled *A Summary View of the Rights of British America*. There he suggests that the congress send an address to the king explaining the American grievances in the hope that the king will intercede to end the violations of "those rights which god and the laws have given equally and independently to all."[1] Jefferson takes surprisingly little time to develop the notion of natural rights and to explain what those rights are and how they

1. *TJ*, I, 121.

belong to the Americans. Like the other major American authors of the period, he appears to take the goal of government as a question that requires no argument. His purpose is to demonstrate how actions of the British government are endangering the achievement of that goal.

What discussion of the rights of human beings there is in *Summary View* is contained in Jefferson's explanation of the origin of the colonies and their governments. He suggests that the petition to the king trace Americans' rights back through colonial history in order to show the solidity of the colonists' claims. The rights given equally and independently to each human being include a right of "departing from the country in which chance, not choice has placed them, of going in quest of new habitations, and of there establishing new societies, under such laws and regulations as to them shall seem most likely to promote public happiness." It was through the exercise of this right to self-determination that the American colonies were originally formed. Jefferson argues that when the Americans migrated, they were free to establish for themselves any government they chose. They chose to establish the system of laws under which they had lived in the mother country, and they chose also to submit themselves to the English monarch, "who was thereby made the central link connecting the several parts of the empire thus newly multiplied." Thus the king is the servant of the people. His authority is derived from their consent, and he is "consequently subject to their superintendence."[2]

The Parliament, on the other hand, was never granted any authority over the American colonists. Jefferson writes that during the period when the colonies were being settled, the Parliament did assist them in defending themselves against an enemy. That assistance, however, was undertaken because it was in the interest of Britain to maintain the advantages of her commerce with the colonies. It did not bind the colonies in any way to the rule of Parliament. Parliament had aided other sovereign nations for similar reasons, and those nations did not, by accepting that aid, lose their sovereignty. Had Parliament made assisting the colonies in their defense contingent upon the colonies' submitting themselves to parliamentary sovereignty, writes Jefferson, the colonists "would have rejected [such terms] with disdain, and trusted for better to the moderation of their enemies, or to a vigorous exertion of their own force."[3]

2. *TJ*, I, 121, 122–23, 121.
3. *TJ*, I, 122.

Nor does Jefferson believe that the fact that Parliament had passed laws regulating trade—laws the Americans had obeyed—constitute evidence of a parliamentary authority over the colonies. Others among the colonial leaders had explained such apparent precedents for parliamentary rule by looking to contracts between the Americans and the British to allow regulation of trade by Parliament. For Jefferson, although it is a fact that the Parliament had regulated colonial trade, it is also a fact that it had never done so legitimately. "The exercise of a free trade with all parts of the world, possessed by the American colonists as of natural right, and which no law of their own had taken away or abridged, was the next object of unjust encroachment." Thus, Parliament passed laws prohibiting the colonists from trading with parts of the world other than Great Britain. It also passed laws prohibiting certain manufacturing in the colonies: "By an act passed in the 5th. year of the reign of his majesty king George the second an American subject is forbidden to make a hat for himself of the fur which he has taken perhaps on his own soil. An instance of despotism to which no parallel can be produced in the most arbitrary ages of British history."[4]

Jefferson's recitation of parliamentary usurpations in the past seems to have at least two objects. One is to argue that the precedents in American history for Parliament's ruling the colonies do not establish the legitimacy of that rule but demonstrate the unjust use of power. The other is to show why it is necessary that Parliament not rule the Americans if the Americans are to preserve their natural rights. "History has informed us that bodies of men as well as individuals are susceptible to the spirit of tyranny."[5] Specifically, the case of Parliament's illegitimate legislation regarding the colonies makes the point. Because the members of Parliament are not affected by the laws they make for the colonies, except to benefit from the unjust restrictions placed upon the Americans' rights, those members have been willing to tyrannize over the colonists. A people with a prudent regard for their rights will understand that it is dangerous to give authority to a legislature whose members are not part of their own community. History demonstrates that such legislatures will be unjust.

Having listed the various parliamentary usurpations that have occurred over the years, Jefferson writes: "We do not point out to his majesty the injustice of these acts with intent to rest on that principle

4. *TJ*, I, 123, 124–25.
5. *TJ*, I, 124.

the cause of their nullity, but to shew that experience confirms the propriety of those political principles which exempt us from the jurisdiction of the British parliament. The true ground on which we declare these acts void is that the British parliament has no right to exercise authority over us."[6] The past and present acts of Parliament regulating the American colonies are illegitimate not because the individual acts violate rights but because no legislature can have authority over a people who are not represented therein. Such a legislature would almost certainly violate people's rights. Jefferson then reaches a conclusion that had become a familiar one in the political thought of the Americans during the years leading to the Revolution: Parliament cannot legislate for the colonies since the colonists are not represented in that body. He reaches that conclusion through a historical and logical demonstration of why representation is critical to the maintenance of the people's rights.

These past violations of American rights through parliamentary legislation, Jefferson continues, were "less alarming" than the violations witnessed in the previous decade. They never resulted in the same kind of crisis between the colonies and the mother country because they were "repeated at more distant intervals, than that rapid and bold succession of injuries which is likely to distinguish the present from all other periods of American story." In recent years the colonies have been afflicted by the Sugar Act, the Stamp Act, the Declaratory Act, the Townshend Acts, the suspension of the New York legislature, and the Coercive Acts. Jefferson continues: "Scarcely have our minds been able to emerge from the astonishment into which one stroke of parliamentary thunder has involved us, before another more heavy and more alarming is fallen on us. Single acts of tyranny may be ascribed to the accidental opinion of a day; but a series of oppressions, begun at a distinguished period, and pursued unalterably thro' every change of ministers, too plainly prove a deliberate, systematical plan of reducing us to slavery."[7]

In discussing the tyrannical nature of these recent acts of Parliament, Jefferson concentrates primarily upon the newest parliamentary assault, the Coercive Acts. These were laws passed by Parliament in 1774 to punish Boston for the Boston Tea Party. One closed the Boston port until such time as Bostonians paid for the destroyed tea. Another took away from the Massachusetts General Assembly the authority to appoint the Council (which served as the upper

6. *TJ*, I, 125.
7. *TJ*, I, 125.

house of the legislature and also possessed some executive and judicial powers) and lodged that authority in the king. A third allowed officials charged with capital offenses to be removed to Britain or to Nova Scotia for trial. And a fourth provided for the quartering of British troops in private homes.

Jefferson's treatment of the acts of the decade preceding 1774 is notable because it does not concentrate upon the various pieces of tax legislation. Instead he gives special attention to the suspension of the New York legislature, an act whereby "one free and independent legislature hereby takes upon itself to suspend the powers of another, free and independent as itself."[8] This act, according to Jefferson, violates both common sense and human nature: it denies to Americans their independence as human beings by allowing the 160,000 electors in Great Britain to give law to the 4,000,000 in America.

Jefferson's choice to concentrate upon this act and not upon the various taxation acts demonstrates his conviction that the real issue between Britain and America is not property as such but the right to control property and the other aspects of human life. The taxation acts sought to take away property without consent. The act suspending the New York legislature is more serious because it removes the people's system for controlling their own lives. Both acts are dangerous manifestations of parliamentary power, but the second is a more direct and ominous assertion that the Americans may not rule themselves, may not exercise their natural right to liberty or self-determination. The taxation acts violated that principle of self-determination, but the suspension of the legislature rejected it. That principle had been rejected clearly by Parliament in the Declaratory Act and just as clearly, it seems to Jefferson, in the act in question. A year later he put it this way: "By one act they have suspended the powers of one American legislature & by another have declared they may legislate for us themselves in all cases whatsoever. these two acts alone form a basis broad enough whereon to erect a despotism of unlimited extent."[9]

One interesting aspect of *Summary View* is that it is the first major work by a major American political thinker of the period to concentrate upon the king and not merely upon Parliament. Jefferson's discussion of parliamentary usurpation is in the form of a suggestion for a petition to the king. His criticisms of Parliament are ultimately criticisms of the king. This approach makes sense because of Jeffer-

8. *TJ*, I, 126.
9. *TJ*, I, 195.

son's claim that the Americans were legitimately ruled never by Parliament but only by the king and their own legislatures. Complaints about abuse of legitimate power cannot be addressed to Parliament precisely because Parliament has no legitimate power over the colonists. Such complaints must be addressed to the king because of his cooperation with Parliament and his failure to protect the colonists from Parliament's tyranny.

Following his discussion of the acts of Parliament of which the king ought to be reminded, Jefferson proceeds to "consider the conduct of his majesty" in order to "mark out his deviations from the line of duty." The first such deviation is the king's failure to protect the Americans from Parliament. Jefferson notes that the king owns a veto power over acts that have passed both houses of Parliament. He also notes that the power has not been used for several generations because kings have not been willing to substitute their wills for that of the legislature. However, he continues, with the addition of "new states to the British empire," it has become irresponsible of the king not to use his veto when Parliament passes legislation that harms the interests of some parts of the empire in order to aid other parts. "It is now therefore the great office of his majesty to resume the exercise of his negative power, and to prevent the passage of laws by any one legislature of the empire which might bear injuriously on the rights and interests of another." Thus Jefferson makes the complaints against Parliament into complaints against the king, who had the authority and responsibility to protect the colonists from the injustice of Parliament but failed to do so. This is far and away the most important of the grievances against the king that Jefferson offers in *Summary View*. Its importance is signaled by the fact that it is the only grievance that Jefferson repeats in his final paragraph in which he exhorts the king to act well toward the colonies: "Only aim at your duty, and mankind will give you credit where you fail. No longer persevere in sacrificing the rights of one part of the empire to the inordinate desires of another: but deal out to all equal and impartial right. Let no act be passed by any one legislature which may infringe on the rights and liberties of another."[10]

Jefferson's other complaints against the king are of two sorts. There are grievances that, like the major one, criticize the king not for his actions but for inactions that lead to the colonists' rights being insecure. Thus Jefferson suggests that the king be reminded that with "inattention to the necessities of his people here, has his majesty

10. *TJ,* I, 129, 134.

permitted our laws to lie neglected in England for years, neither confirming them by his assent, nor annulling them by his negative."[11] In
a similar vein, Jefferson criticizes the king for not acting through the
colonial governors to call new legislatures into session when they are
needed. The other grievances have to do with actions by the king that
are dangerous to the rights of the colonists. Jefferson complains that
the king, unwilling to use his veto with Parliament, is more than
willing to negate acts of colonial legislatures despite the fact that the
acts vetoed might be very beneficial to the colonists. He also discusses the king's ordering that colonial legislatures be dissolved, his
instruction that Virginia counties not be divided unless the new
county agree to have no representative in the colonial assembly, his
dissolving of legislative bodies, and his sending of armed troops to the
colonies.

Most of the grievances Jefferson offers against the king are not
about actions of the king that directly violate colonial rights. With
the obvious exception of the complaint about troops being sent to the
colonies without their consent, Jefferson's complaints concentrate
upon the king's failure to protect rights from other threats—notably
threats from Parliament—and upon actions or inactions by the king
that make his government ineffective in promoting public happiness.
Jefferson writes that the king "is no more than the chief officer of the
people, appointed by the laws, and circumscribed with definite
powers, to assist in working the great machine of government erected
for their use."[12] Most especially, the people use government to protect their liberty. But government under the king is failing to accomplish that task, and for that reason, Jefferson suggests in his final
paragraph, the Americans may have to exercise their natural right to
self-determination and separate themselves from his majesty's rule.

Two years after Jefferson wrote *Summary View*, the Americans did
exercise their right to self-determination when they declared themselves independent of Great Britain. After the Continental Congress
decided for independence, its members approved a document explaining the reasons for their actions. That document had been prepared in the preceding weeks by a committee whose members had
delegated to Thomas Jefferson the task of preparing the draft. The
draft was altered in some of its language by other members of the
committee as well as by the congress, but the alterations were such as
to create a declaration that remained clearly Jefferson's work. Thus

11. *TJ*, I, 130.
12. *TJ*, I, 121.

Jefferson became the author of the document most closely associated with the American revolutionaries, the Declaration of Independence.

The virtue of the Declaration of Independence does not lie in any original political analysis. The purpose of the document is to state the beliefs that the Americans held in common and not to go beyond those beliefs. Thus Jefferson later explained that his objective in writing it was:

> Not to find out new principles, or new arguments, never before thought of, not merely to say things which had never been said before; but to place before mankind the common sense of the subject, in terms so plain and firm as to command their assent. . . . Neither aiming at originality of principles or sentiments, nor yet copied from any particular and previous writing, it was intended to be an expression of the American mind. . . . All its authority rests on the harmonizing sentiments of the day, whether expressed in conversation, in letters, printed essays, or the elementary books of public right, as Aristotle, Cicero, Locke, Sidney, etc.[13]

Jefferson states those harmonizing sentiments in a succinct and clear way. The virtue of the Declaration derives from Jefferson's ability to understand and to voice the American mind.

The Declaration of Independence begins with a statement of political principles—a statement of what makes government just. It proceeds to its most lengthy part, an application of those principles to the government of George III over the colonies. It then closes with the formal declaration that the American colonies are henceforth free and independent states. The best-known part is the first:

> We hold these truths to be self-evident, that all men are created equal, that they are endowed by their Creator with certain unalienable Rights, that among these are Life, Liberty, and the pursuit of Happiness.—That to secure these rights, Governments are instituted among Men, deriving their just powers from the consent of the governed,—That whenever any Form of Government becomes destructive of these ends, it is the Right of the People to alter or abolish it, and to institute new Government, laying its foundation on such principles and organizing its powers in such form, as to them shall seem most likely to effect their Safety and Happiness.

Jefferson thus states in very compact form the natural rights doctrine that lay behind the major American revolutionaries' arguments. The clarity of that doctrine in the minds of the Americans is indi-

13. Carl L. Becker, *The Declaration of Independence* (New York, 1942), 25–26.

cated by the first phrase. The statement that "we hold these truths to be self-evident" (originally Jefferson wrote "sacred and undeniable") indicates that to the colonists the principled argument is well known and widely accepted.[14] Its evidence does not need to be offered, for anyone with a clear, rational mind can understand its truth. That the principles of natural rights were a basic part of the American mind is also indicated by the fact that Jefferson did not state them in *Summary View:* there was no need to instruct delegates to the Congress about things that were self-evident to them and to their fellow countrymen.

For the purposes of the Declaration, the most important of the self-evident truths is the last one: that the people have a right to abolish a government and establish a new one when the government does not do its job. That is exactly what the Americans were doing at the time, and the Declaration seeks to explain the justice of that act. But the conclusion that people may revolt follows from the other truths—the truths about what the job of governments is or about what governments must fail to do in order for the people to have a right to revolt.

The explanation of why the people have a right to revolt begins with facts about human nature. Human beings are created equal (originally Jefferson wrote "equal & independent"). The self-evident equality of human beings could not lie in strength, in beauty, in intellectual ability, or in wealth, but must lie in the simple fact of their humanity, of their belonging to the same species. There is something in human beings that makes them all human beings, that makes them all fundamentally the same. This fundamental sameness means that it is not clear that any human being has a right to rule another: nature sets up social hierarchies for ants and bees but not for human beings.

Natural equality and independence from rule result in human beings' having certain rights. That is, there are things that human beings are morally permitted to do according to their nature. Since each is naturally on his own, each is morally allowed to take care of himself: to do what is necessary to maintain his life, to maintain his liberty—his natural freedom from rule by others—and to pursue his own happiness. The fact that all human beings are morally free to act as they think necessary for these ends, however, does not result in a

14. Jefferson's original draft, as well as the draft submitted to the Congress, can be found in Becker, *Declaration of Independence,* 141–51, 160–71.

circumstance in which human beings' lives, liberty, and pursuit of happiness are guaranteed. When human beings decide for themselves, independent of each other, what is useful for these ends, they tend to get in one another's way. What is seen as necessary for one to preserve his life may restrict the liberty of another. Thus, in a state of nature, though each has rights, it is likely that the rights of none will be secure.

Jefferson's understanding that equal rights do not at all guarantee secure rights is expressed in the passage that says, "to secure these rights governments are instituted among men." Human beings, naturally independent from rule, reach the conclusion that without some form of common rule their rights will not be secure from one another. They make a contract, each choosing to give up some of his right to judge for himself what is necessary for life, liberty, and the pursuit of happiness, so long as the others give up the same. They form a government to which they give the task of enforcing the contract so that the rights of each may be more secure than they would otherwise be. This government only has certain authority—the authority that the people decide to give it in order to secure their rights. Thus governments derive "their just powers from the consent of the governed." It could be no other way, for people being naturally equal and having a right to liberty, it follows that they could never be morally obliged to obey another unless they had agreed to obey that other. They make that agreement because they see it as the most effective means for securing their rights.

According to these self-evident truths, then, legitimate government must be created by the consent of the governed and must act to secure individual rights. When government acts outside the bounds defined by the people's consent or when it acts to endanger rather than to secure individual rights, the people may change it or replace it in order better to provide for their "safety and happiness," which cannot be realized unless government secures individual rights effectively.

The Declaration of Independence contains no argument that kingships are inherently bad. Its argument is that kings must remain within the boundaries given them by the people and that within those boundaries they must use their authority to secure individual rights. The bulk of the document is devoted not to establishing that point—it is self-evident—but to demonstrating that King George III has repeatedly exceeded his legitimate authority and that he has failed to secure individual rights effectively. Only by showing that George III is a bad king can the Americans show the justice of their rejection of British rule.

The list of grievances is long, and all the grievances are against the king. The word *Parliament* is not to be found in the Declaration because the colonists were not revolting from Parliament for the simple reason that they believed Parliament had never ruled them legitimately. The grievance list was not difficult to construct. It contains most of the things Jefferson had discussed in *Summary View*, and much of it is copied from Jefferson's draft of a constitution for Virginia written a month before the Declaration. It contains the issues that the intellectual leaders of the American Revolution had been discussing for the previous decade: the various taxation acts, the Declaratory Act, the Quartering Act, the payment of judicial salaries by the government in London, the suspension of the New York legislature, the restrictions on jury trials with the extension of the authority of the admiralty courts, the Coercive Acts, and the stationing of British troops in the colonies.

Many of the grievances against the king are, like those in *Summary View*, concerned not with directly tyrannical acts but with the failure or refusal on the king's part to use his powers to secure American rights effectively. The first on the list, for example, is that "he has refused his assent to laws the most wholesome and necessary for the public good." In that way the king has failed to act well to secure the right to pursue happiness. Others, like the stationing of troops in the colonies, the waging of war against the colonists, and the exciting of domestic insurrections, are acts that violate individual rights more directly. These latter are cases in which the king has gone beyond his legitimate powers as consented to by the people.

The most important grievance to speak of the king's going beyond his legitimate powers is also the longest of the grievances: "He has combined with others to subject us to a jurisdiction foreign to our constitution and unacknowledged by our laws, giving his Assent to their Acts of pretended Legislation." Here is the critical issue of the revolutionary period, the authority of Parliament. The king has allowed and encouraged a legislature that the Americans have not agreed to obey to make laws to control the behavior of Americans. Many of those laws had sought to change colonial government in order to take away from the people of the colonies the ability to govern themselves and to resist control from London. The more serious violation of colonial rights, however, is the simple fact of parliamentary legislation. The colonists did not understand themselves to have consented to rule by Parliament. Neither in their charters nor in their laws is assent to rule by Parliament to be found. In supporting parliamentary legislation with regard to the Americans, then, the king denies that government must be based upon consent. He removes the Americans' security that they are in control of their lives and liberties and that they may pursue happiness according to rules they create themselves or have consented to.

Following the general statement of the king's complicity with Parliament in subjecting the colonists to the rule of a legislature to which they have not consented, the Declaration lists nine particular "acts of pretended legislation." Fourth in that list is "imposing taxes on us without our consent." That Jefferson gives this particular grievance an undistinguished place in the list indicates his agreement with the arguments made by the other great leaders of the revolutionary period. The colonial concern with the Stamp Act, the Townshend Acts, and the Tea Act was not the narrow, pragmatic fear of losing more income in taxes. The concern always centered on the fundamental political principle of Parliament's authority to tax the colonists without their consent. Such action was not allowed by the British constitution or by colonial charters or laws. For that reason, in taxing the colonists Parliament presented the grave threat that it could indeed do anything it chose to the Americans and that, therefore, the Americans were not free to determine their own lives.

Jefferson's argument in *Summary View* also indicates that for him the fundamental issue between Britain and the colonies is not property but self-determination. This belief is further shown, perhaps more subtly, in Jefferson's statement of principles in the Declaration of Independence. The unalienable rights of human beings he chooses to list are life, liberty, and the pursuit of happiness. The more usual list, both in the works of the political philosophers most influential among the revolutionaries and among the leading revolutionaries themselves, was made up of life, liberty, and property. By writing of the right to pursue happiness in place of the right to property, Jefferson demonstrates his and his colleagues' belief that what is important is the colonists' liberty to do what they believe necessary and useful with their lives. Secure property is surely something needed for a person to pursue happiness, but it may not be the only means or even the most important one. Taxing people without their consent violates their right to pursue happiness because they cannot know when the government will frustrate that pursuit by removing their property. At stake here is not the property itself but the importance of controlling one's own property along with the other aspects of one's life. Without such control it is meaningless to speak of the individual pursuit of happiness.

The Declaration of Independence has a clear, logical purpose and form. It states the principles of politics. It lists violations of those principles by the king of Great Britain. It declares that the Americans are free from the rule of the king because of those violations. But in the midst of this explanation of the justice of American independence, there is much that is said about human nature and the role of politics in human life, more specifically, about the meaning of liberty for human beings and their happiness.

The most basic assumption behind the Declaration is that human beings are rational. They can make decisions about what is sensible and just, and they can live according to those decisions. The document begins:

> When in the Course of human events, it becomes necessary for one people to dissolve the political bands, that have connected them with another, and to assume among the powers of the earth, the separate and equal station to which the Laws of Nature and of Nature's God entitle them, a decent respect to the opinions of mankind requires that they should declare the causes which impel them to the separation.

Jefferson addresses himself to human rationality, to that which makes the opinions of mankind respectable. As the principles he goes on to state make clear, reasonable people understand that government is necessary for human beings. They also understand, therefore, that the rejection of a government is a very serious act, one that requires careful consideration. In the Declaration, Jefferson seeks to make that careful consideration manifest. He attempts to show that the American rejection of British rule is not an insult to human reason, and therefore to human dignity, but a decision that comes from and seeks to maintain human beings' rational capacity.

The understanding that because revolution is dangerous it must be based upon a reasonable understanding of political principles and circumstances appears in many passages in the Declaration. Following the statement of self-evident truths, Jefferson rushes to note that "prudence, indeed, will dictate that Governments long established should not be changed for light and transient causes." Reasonable people understand that no government can be perfect and that all governments will err at times. There appears to be an assumption here that long-standing governments are more likely to be good than bad. Underlying that assumption is the belief that rational human beings would not allow a government to continue in power were it fundamentally bad. Just as the American people are now acting reasonably to maintain the security of their rights by changing their government, so before the present crisis they acted reasonably to secure their rights by maintaining British rule. This point is also made in *Summary View*, where Jefferson lists parliamentary usurpations from the years preceding the revolutionary crisis but explains that none of these previous violations of colonial rights was serious enough to warrant revolution.

The Americans' conviction that their government had once been a good one, worthy of support despite occasional injustices, is registered elsewhere in the Declaration. After the list of grievances, Jefferson writes that "in every stage of these Oppressions We have Petitioned for Redress in the most humble terms: Our repeated Petitions have been answered only by repeated injury." In other words, Jefferson says that the Americans attempted to appeal to the king's reason in the hope that the good government they had enjoyed before the 1760s would be restored, so that their government would not have to be changed and all the dangers that such a change involves could be avoided.

Indeed, writes Jefferson, the Americans appealed not only to the reason of the king but also to that of the British people:

> Nor have We been wanting in our attentions to our British brethren. We have warned them from time to time of attempts by their legislature to extend an unwarrantable jurisdiction over us. We have reminded them of the circumstances of our emigration and settlement here. We have appealed to their native justice and magnanimity, and we have conjured them by the ties of our common kindred to disavow these usurpations, which would inevitably interrupt our connections and correspondence. They too have been deaf to the voice of justice and consanguinity.

Thus, assuming that the British people are ultimately responsible for their own government and that they have supported it because it has been good, the Americans appealed to those people to make their government act as it ought. They too, however, have refused to act reasonably. They have failed to constrain their government to act according to what is self-evidently the truth about the purpose of government.

In treating his readers as rational creatures and in explaining that the Americans have treated the king and the British people as reasonable creatures, Jefferson indicates the issue that has led the Americans to declare independence: they expect to be treated as rational creatures. Liberty is essential for human beings in order for them to have the opportunity to exercise this characteristically human capacity to be rational. The great problem with the actions of the British over the previous decade was that they tended to prohibit to the Americans this opportunity to control themselves through decisions made with their own minds. They tended to dehumanize the Americans. The pursuit of liberty is not primarily the pursuit of property but the pursuit of human dignity.

The connection between freedom and dignity comes through with clarity in *Summary View*. There Jefferson suggests that the Continental Congress remind the king of this important connection: "That these are our grievances which we have thus laid before his majesty with that freedom of language and sentiment which becomes a free people, claiming their rights as derived from the laws of nature, and not as the gift of their chief magistrate. Let those flatter, who fear: it is not an American art. To give praise where it is not due, might be well from the venal, but would ill beseem those who are asserting the rights of human nature."[15] Liberty and reason go together. Liberty is the rightful possession of human beings because nature made them rational. In seeking the security of liberty, then, human beings ought to act like rational beings by speaking the truth and by demanding what is their right. They must maintain a dignity suited to their natural station.

The alternative to maintaining liberty, for Jefferson, is to become something less than human. In a 1775 letter to John Randolph, he wrote that "we must drub [the British] soundly before the sceptered tyrant will know we are not mere brutes, to crouch under his hand and kiss the rod with which he deigns to scourge us."[16] Human beings use their rational capacity to decide how they will live their lives. Without the liberty for self-determination, they become subhuman. It is according to the law of nature, which makes human beings what they are, then, that they have liberty.

In the Declaration Jefferson writes of "the necessity which constrains them to alter their former Systems of Government." This is one of three places in the Declaration where he characterizes the

15. *TJ*, I, 134.
16. *TJ*, I, 270.

American action as necessary. The necessity is one derived from nature. If the Americans are to remain fully human, they must be able to determine their own lives. Since the evidence of recent years indicates that the British government cannot be counted on to provide that liberty, it is indeed necessary to throw off that government.[17]

With this understanding of the necessity of liberty for the fulfillment of human nature, it is possible to explain an aspect of the Declaration of Independence that at first may seem incongruous. The political principles explained in the Declaration are clearly the natural rights teaching of modern political philosophy. This is not at all surprising, for Jefferson is attempting to voice the "American mind," and, as the examinations of Otis, Henry, Dickinson, and the Adamses show, all of the major American political thinkers of the period derive their arguments from that teaching. Even when the Americans base their objections to British policy on arguments about the rights of Englishmen, they make it clear that those rights derive from the natural rights of human beings. The natural rights doctrine puts the emphasis upon human self-interest, upon the claims that individual human beings, according to nature, may do whatever they think necessary to preserve their lives, liberties, and estates. According to this philosophy, civil society is the result of the self-interested decision of each that his rights will be best secured if he agrees to join civil society and obey its laws. Those laws, however, are bound to maintain a certain amount of freedom for the individual to pursue his own interests as he chooses, for it is only in order to be able to do more effectively what he wishes that an individual consents to be governed. Thus the American claims against Britain were that the colonists had not consented to be ruled by Parliament and that, therefore, Parliament could not legitimately take their property or otherwise restrict the colonists' natural right to determine their own lives.

The modern political philosophy stated in the Declaration, then, emphasizes self-interest as opposed to selfless concern about others. It bases civil society upon individual rights—selfish claims—as opposed to duties to other people. Yet there are two passages in the document in which Jefferson speaks of the Americans in terms that

17. Gary Wills writes of Jefferson: "He does not offer the American Revolution as something permissible, merely. It is *necessary* in nature; and the recognition and cooperation with nature is the essence of human virtue." Gary Wills, *Inventing America* (Garden City, 1978), 317–18. On the deficiencies of Wills' interpretation of the Declaration, see Gary J. Schmitt, "Sentimental Journey: Gary Wills and the American Founding," *Political Science Reviewer*, XII (Fall, 1982), 99–128.

seem foreign to that political philosophy. The first occurs after the statement that prudence dictates that people should not revolt over small matters. There, Jefferson continues the argument by adding that "when a long train of abuses and usurpations, pursuing invariably the same Object evinces a design to reduce them under absolute Despotism, it is their right, it is their duty, to throw off such Government, and to provide new Guards for their future security." The statement of principles is designed to establish that this right to revolt exists, and the list of grievances is designed to convince the reader that the right is prudently employed in the present case. But here Jefferson goes beyond the language of rights to speak of a duty. Not only may the Americans throw off British government, but somehow they are also obliged to. To have a right is to have an option to act, but to have a duty is to be obliged to act. That obligation, that duty, does not come from contract, which is the source of political obligation according to modern political philosophy, for the obligation is to use a freedom that cannot be contracted away.

The other passage that seems incongruous with the natural rights doctrine of the Declaration is the final phrase. Jefferson writes that for the support of the Declaration the Americans pledge to one another "our Lives, our Fortunes and our sacred Honor." Honor is something that does not usually characterize modern political philosophy, for it is a virtue that leads people to act well toward one another. It is a virtue that leads people to do their duty. It is a motive that differs from the self-interested motives that are assumed and cultivated by modern politics.

The duty and the honor of which Jefferson speaks, however, are not so incongruous with the general philosophy of the Declaration as they might at first appear. They are connected to human beings' rational capacity, from which comes the natural right to liberty. Independence was "necessary," for Jefferson, because British rule would no longer allow the colonists the opportunity to use their native reason to control their own lives. British rule would not allow them to be human. The honor of which Jefferson writes is the honor granted by nature to the Americans of being rational creatures. Their honor as human beings is very much at stake in the Revolution. Their duty to act to secure liberty is an obligation that comes from nature. Without changing their system of government, they cannot maintain the liberty to be free agents using the faculties nature gives them. In order to have the opportunity to fulfill their natures, then, the Americans have a natural obligation to secure their liberty. That obligation, along with the understanding that British actions were a severe threat to the colonists' liberty, is what led Jefferson and his fellow citizens to the decision that the political connection between the colonies and Great Britain "is and ought to be totally dissolved."

SEVEN

Liberty

❧❦❧

John Dickinson stated the issue simply: "We are animated by a just love of our invaded rights."[1] The first conclusion to be reached from a study of the political thought of the leaders of the American Revolution is that the Americans resisted and ultimately revolted against Great Britain in order to secure their liberty. The constant theme in the writings of the great American patriots is that the liberty of the colonists is endangered by the acts of the British government and that the colonists ought to do something to prevent a possession so valuable being eroded away. They were animated, and they animated others, to act to maintain liberty because they felt it and knew it to be something real and of great importance, something not often exercised by human beings in the history of the world, something secured in the past and in the future only with great difficulty.

Niccolo Machiavelli, who was not moved by an ideology created in him by British opposition thinkers of the seventeenth and eighteenth centuries, understood that people could be genuinely dedicated to liberty: "And whoever becomes the master of a city accustomed to living in liberty, and does not destroy it—he waits to be destroyed by it. For it always has a refuge in rebellion in the name of liberty and its ancient orders." The Americans did believe that their liberty was of ancient origin in two ways. First, there was the tradition of liberty belonging to the English people, a tradition that traced back to Magna Carta. That liberty was understood to have been denied at times in British history, but it had always been reestablished, most recently at the time of the Glorious Revolution. Second, there was the strong

1. *PWD*, II, 14.

tradition of liberty in America. The colonists argued consistently that the settlement of the American continent had been undertaken in order that the people emigrating might be able to enjoy their liberty more securely than they had in Europe. They argued that once in North America, the Americans had maintained their allegiance to the British king and with it their rights as Englishmen, indeed, that the citizens of some of the colonies had made contracts with the king in the colonial charters to maintain their liberties. And the Americans believed that until the end of the Seven Years' War those liberties had been secured. They were, to use Machiavelli's words, accustomed to living in liberty. Thus, they understood themselves to be seeking not anything new in the revolutionary period but something old and valuable. As James Otis put it at the beginning of the struggle: "A continuation of the same liberties that have been enjoyed by the colonists since the [Glorious] Revolution, and the same moderation of government exercised towards them will bind them in perpetual lawful and willing subjection, obedience, and love to Great Britain."[2] At the beginning of the dispute the colonists were British, and they loved being British. They had a stronger love, however, for liberty.

There were some in the British Parliament who understood this American love of liberty as the real and strong phenomenon it was. William Pitt summed up the reasons for American resistance in a short sentence: "It is plain that *America* cannot bear chains." Edmund Burke explained to the Parliament in 1775 that "this fierce spirit of liberty is stronger in the English colonies probably than in any other People of the earth." Burke offers six reasons to explain this fact. First, he, like the American authors, traces the American love of liberty to the British heritage. Traditional British liberty not only equipped the colonists with a bias in favor of it, but it also gave them some concrete understanding of things necessary for the maintenance of liberty, most especially that representation is required for taxation to be just. Second, explains Burke, the American habit of liberty has been augmented by the popular form of the American governments. Because of the importance of the popularly elected colonial assemblies, the people are more used to ruling themselves there than elsewhere and are loathe to give up the role. A third factor creating the ardent love of liberty in Americans is religion. Burke agrees with John Adams that Protestant churches are more friendly to

2. Niccolo Machiavelli, *The Prince*, trans. Leo Paul de Alvarez (Irving, Tex., 1980), 30; *JO*, 459.

liberty than the Roman Catholic and Anglican churches, and Burke argues that the reason for this friendliness to liberty is that the Protestant churches began as dissenting churches that depended upon the existence of political and religious liberty for their own existence. A fourth reason for the American love of liberty applies in the South, and that is the existence of the institution of slavery. "Where this is the case in any part of the world those who are free are far the most proud and jealous of their freedom. Freedom to them is not only an enjoyment, but a kind of rank and privilege."[3] That is to say, despite the contradiction where chattel slavery exists among a people dedicated to human liberty, its existence makes freedom appear as a more real and valuable thing by providing a constant reminder of what it means not to be free and by implying a certain superiority for non-slaves over those who are slaves. A fifth factor is education. Burke writes that the Americans are well enough educated to understand the value of freedom as well as the governmental actions that are likely to protect or threaten it. Last, Burke lists the fact that British influence on the colonies has been less direct than elsewhere for the simple reason that it is difficult to rule a people carefully when that people lives three thousand miles and an ocean away. The Americans, therefore, were used to being left alone by the British government.

The American love of liberty was a habit created by the exercise of liberty over the years. Their liberty was a thing experienced and felt, a thing so strongly appreciated that the people would fight for it. That appreciation came partially from the habit and the feeling, but not entirely. It came also from thought, from argument. The threats to the security of liberty during the revolutionary period caused the Americans to think about their accustomed state of liberty and to wonder about what liberty is, why it is of value, and what governmental actions are serious threats to its security. Samuel Adams, for example, wrote in a 1770 address to the lieutenant governor of Massachusetts that "the Rights of the province having been of late years most severely attackd, has inducd Gentlemen to examine the Constitution more thorowly, & has increasd their Zeal in its Defence."[4] The conclusions of such examinations became the arguments of the American patriots to their fellow citizens to explain why liberty is

3. *JD*, xiv; Edmund Burke, *Speeches and Letters on American Affairs* (New York, 1908), 91, 94.
4. *SA*, II, 24.

valuable and how that valuable thing was being threatened by the actions of the British government.

What is this liberty and why is it so valuable? From the arguments of the colonial leaders, it is clear that the liberty they were fighting for involves simply being left alone to control their own lives. It is the freedom from control by an absolute or arbitrary government—a freedom that allows human beings to decide how they will live and what they will and will not do. The absence of liberty is slavery: a circumstance where another human being or group of human beings decides how one will live or what one will or will not do.

The right to liberty was understood by the Americans to be a broad one, including other rights, especially the right to property. Certainly issues of the right to property originated the whole crisis, and such issues continued to arise throughout the revolutionary period. The Americans were never shy in their reactions to the Stamp Act, the Townshend Acts, and the Tea Act about expressing their desire and right to protect their own property against British taxation. In each case the colonists argued that the Parliament was violating their rights by attempting to take their property without their consent.

This right not to be taxed without consent, which was understood to be, in the words of the Virginia Resolves, "the distinguishing Characteristic of *British* FREEDOM," was defended by both Samuel Adams and James Otis. They based their arguments upon John Locke's argument that private property exists by right in a state of nature and can be justly taken from a person even in civil society only with his consent. Otis writes: "In a state of nature no man can take my property from me without my consent: if he does he deprives me of my liberty and makes me a slave. If such a proceeding is a breach of the law of nature, no law of society can make it just." The violation of liberty in this case is simple and clear. When the fruits of a person's labor are at the complete disposition of another, then that person does not work for himself to determine his own life and gain the rewards from his own activity but works, indeed as a slave, for another. It is from this observation that John Dickinson's reminder that "we cannot enjoy Liberty without Property" follows.[5] Without some assurance of material sufficiency, a human being cannot plan for the future and decide how he wishes to live his life. He has no freedom for self-determination.

5. *JO,* 447; *JD,* 16.

The Americans argued also that taxation without representation violated their liberty in other ways. The direct violations of the right to property were seen by none of the revolutionary leaders as the prime danger to liberty threatened by the various acts passed by the Parliament during the period before the Revolution. The more imposing spectacle was not the thought of having to render money in taxes but the idea of the way in which those taxes were legislated. The issue began as an issue over the right to property, but it quickly became the far broader and more serious issue of absolute, arbitrary governmental power. When the colonists objected to the Stamp Act with the argument that a legislature in which they were not represented had no authority to tax them, the British government began to assert an authority to rule the Americans absolutely.[6] Thereafter Parliament's claim—as stated in the 1766 Declaratory Act—that it had the authority "to make laws . . . to bind the Colonists and People of America . . . in all Cases whatsoever" became the ground of the dispute between the colonists and the mother country. It was this fundamental issue of the authority of Parliament to rule the Americans that presented the most serious, and most dangerous, specter to the colonists. The money that they would have had to spend in taxes in order to obey the Stamp Act, the Townshend Acts, and the Tea Act was never great, but the danger of parliamentary tyranny always seemed so.[7] In the words of Edmund Burke, "Men may lose little in property by the act which takes away all their freedom."[8]

Through the use of Montesquieu's definition of liberty as a "tranquility of mind arising from the opinion which each man has of his own safety," Samuel Adams frequently pointed to the danger involved in Parliament's assertion of absolute authority. Its assertion of authority to do all things in the Declaratory Act and its attempts to implement that authority in subsequent years had the tendency to remove any such opinion of safety. If Parliament could do anything it chose to the colonists, then those colonists had no security whatever for their property or their liberty—they had no dependable latitude

6. See Robert W. Tucker and David C. Hendrickson, *The Fall of the First British Empire* (Baltimore, 1982), 147.

7. Bernhard Knollenberg points out that for publishers of newspapers the Stamp duties could have been quite burdensome. Bernhard Knollenberg, *Growth of the American Revolution 1766–1775* (New York, 1975), 49. He also makes it clear, however, that the colonists' major concern about the Stamp Act was that it would serve as a precedent for other parliamentary taxation of them. See Bernhard Knollenberg, *Origin of the American Revolution* (New York, 1960), esp. 225, 236–37.

8. Burke, *American Affairs*, 121.

within which they might be in control of themselves. The security of the right to liberty demands limits on government and some popular check to make sure those limits are obeyed. Neither of these two could be present for the colonists if Parliament was to be able to govern them in all cases whatsoever. John Dickinson summarized the problem simply by writing that there could be no better definition of slavery than Parliament's words in the Declaratory Act.[9]

The threat of absolute, arbitrary government was posed by the various revenue acts passed by Parliament during the revolutionary period but certainly not only by those acts. There were threats to the system of trial by a jury of one's peers that came with the extension of the jurisdiction of the admiralty courts and in the acts requiring those accused of certain crimes to be tried in England rather than in the colonies. There were the attempts to alter the people's ability to control colonial governments by taking away the colonial assemblies' authority to pay the salaries of governors and judges and by having those salaries paid instead by the government in London. There was the bold assertion by Parliament of its authority, in effect, to demolish colonial legislatures when it ordered the legislature of New York suspended until that body obeyed the Quartering Act. There was the stationing of British soldiers in the colonies. Finally, there were the Coercive Acts. To a people used to controlling their own lives in all matters but trade, all of these acts by the British legislature created a legitimate and profound fear that their lives were no longer to be their own—that they would no longer exercise decisive influence over what they did and did not do.

The writings of the thoughtful leaders of the American Revolution express constantly the fear that their cherished liberty is continually being assaulted by Parliament. These quotations from the works of John Dickinson, Samuel Adams, and John Adams, discussed earlier, in combination here show the convergence of the revolutionaries' ideas:

> Is it possible to form an idea of slavery more *compleat*, more *miserable*, more *disgraceful*, than that of a people where *justice is administered*, *government exercised*, and a *standing army maintained*, AT THE EXPENCE OF THE PEOPLE, and yet WITHOUT THE LEAST DEPENDENCE UPON THEM?

> This measure [crown payment of judicial salaries] would complete the Tragedy of American Freedom, for [the people] could conceive of no

9. *SA*, I, 37; *PWD*, I, 311.

state of slavery more perfect, than for Parliament in which they could have no voice to claim a power of making laws to bind them in all cases whatever, and to exercise that assumed Power in taking their money from them and appropriating it for the support of Judges who are to execute such laws as that parliament should see fit to make binding upon them, and a Fleet and Army to enforce their subjection to them.

They [the people of Massachusetts] uniformly think that the destruction of their charter, making the council and judges wholly dependent upon the crown, and the people subjected to the unlimited power of parliament as their supreme legislative, is slavery.[10]

Statements such as these in the literature of American resistance must be taken seriously as reliable indicators of what the American Revolution was all about. One cannot appreciate the Revolution without understanding that the Americans' desire for liberty—their desire not to be as slaves, completely in the control of others—was real and very strongly felt. Perhaps the strongest indication of this fact is the reaction of the people of the colonies to the Virginia Resolves. Those resolves were not oratory couched in flowery, passionate language but a bold, straightforward assertion that the Americans had a right to liberty. The colonists' agreement with that assertion, the strength with which they held their conviction, and the importance they attached to that liberty they believed to be theirs by right were registered in their positive reaction to the resolves. American resistance and revolution was caused by a fear that liberty was about to be lost.

The Americans' habitual love of liberty was what lay behind their actions during the revolutionary period. It would be misleading, however, to suggest that the American concern for liberty was based only upon feeling and habit. It was based upon rational argument as well. The period of resistance leading to the Revolution made the colonists think carefully about their lives and the role that politics ought to play in them. It made them wonder about their love of liberty—about whether that love ought to be as strong as it was, about whether liberty is indeed something important enough to be willing to fight for, and about what kinds of governmental actions provide serious threats to liberty. These reflections on the meaning and importance of liberty can be seen clearly in the writings of the American patriot leaders.

When Jefferson writes in the *Summary View* that Americans are

10. *JD*, 372; *SA*, III, 85; *JA*, IV, 54.

"claiming their rights as derived from the laws of nature," he is expressing an understanding of the source of the right to liberty that was shared by all major American thinkers of the revolutionary period. At the beginning of that period, James Otis wrote of the importance of maintaining liberty in these words: "Rescued human nature must and will be from the general slavery that has so long triumphed over the species." Similarly, Samuel Adams agreed that liberty is a right belonging to human beings because "every man is born naturally free." John Adams argued that "an enemy to liberty" is "an enemy to human nature." John Dickinson found the love of liberty to be "natural to the human heart."[11]

The American thinkers are in agreement, then, that it is according to nature for human beings to have the opportunity to make the choices that determine their own lives. Human beings as human are possessed of liberty. Human beings under the control of others—slaves—are incompletely human since they do not control their own lives. Those who considered the naturalness of liberty for human beings further, especially John Adams and John Dickinson, indicate in their discussions of liberty what it is about human beings that makes them naturally free. Adams and Dickinson argue that it is right for human beings to have the opportunity to make choices because they have the ability to make choices. Dickinson frequently makes a connection between the exercise of liberty and rational behavior, and he does so most often when he is exhorting his fellow citizens to act responsibly in pursuit of liberty. He encourages them to act to maintain the exercise of this natural right but also to act prudently, moderately, without rage in order that "all mankind must, with unceasing applauses, confess that YOU indeed DESERVE liberty."[12] Dickinson does not mean here that liberty is a privilege to be granted to human beings by other human beings only after some demonstration of merit, but rather he means that liberty is a right that inheres in human beings because they are rational. He challenges others to exercise that right responsibly, to use their natural faculty of reason in securing their right to use that same faculty, and thus to demonstrate why it is that liberty is natural to human beings. It is logical to conclude that nature has made human beings free—has given the species a privilege it has not given to other species—from the premise that nature has made human beings rational. It would make no sense to argue that nature gives human beings the ability to

11. *TJ*, I, 134; *JO*, 459; *SA*, II, 258; *JA* III, 470; *JD*, 353.
12. *JD*, 406.

decide what is advantageous and what not, but not the opportunity to use that faculty.

John Adams too derives human beings' natural right to liberty from their rational capacity. Dickinson's argument—that if the colonists had been kept ignorant they would not have developed the strong love of liberty that comes with the development of the ability to exercise the rational faculty—is corroborated by the argument Adams makes. He says that for centuries men were prevented from agitating for liberty by religious and political rulers who followed a policy of keeping them ignorant in order to avoid their understanding their right to liberty. Liberty and rationality are intimately connected: the development of each allows and encourages the development of the other. Only with the development of both is the fullness of human nature realized. Adams writes that governments that allow liberty, and with it the use of human reason by ordinary people in the course of day-to-day living, are governments "agreeable to the dignity of human nature."[13]

The Americans, then, not only felt but *understood* that liberty is a thing to be valued highly. However, the Americans also understood that the fact that all human beings ought to be free does not mean that all human beings are rational enough to be capable of ruling themselves or that all human beings are human enough to be able to use reason to rule themselves. Adams makes the point by noticing that absolute government was needed at one time for civilizing a barbarous people.[14] But once civilized, once made rational, people have the right as human beings to rule themselves and to make their own decisions. They even have a right to be wrong about what will bring them happiness. Jefferson makes the point by writing that government exists to secure the people's right to pursue happiness. Government on its own is simply incapable of making people happy because happiness requires the development of the faculties of a human being. Human beings left to themselves may make poor choices, but without the opportunity to make choices for themselves they cannot be happy. Once the people in a society develop some rational capacity, they can become actually—not merely potentially—human, and to become human they must be granted the exercise of their natural right to liberty. Obviously it would be a difficult problem to say what test might be employed to determine that a people had developed sufficient rational capacity to be able to rule themselves.

13. *JA*, III, 453.
14. *JA*, 450.

For the Americans' purpose it was enough to note that they had become sufficiently rational to exercise their natural liberty, and Dickinson's exhortations to his fellow citizens are meant to persuade them to remind the world of this fact through their actions. This grant of the exercise of the natural right to liberty, however, is one the Americans understood to have been given rarely in history. As Otis puts it, the human species has been kept in subjection throughout human history and with that subjection has been kept in a subhuman state.

The Americans believed that the British in both the old and new worlds had replaced that subjection with freedom and had made it possible for human beings to become more fully human than ever before by allowing them the opportunity to develop and use their rational abilities. It followed from the understanding of the critical importance of liberty for human beings that it was crucially important that the great gains made under British rule by humanity not be lost. From this calculation arise the frequently made statements in the writings of the colonial political thinkers about the responsibility of the Americans to maintain liberty for their posterity. When John Adams claims that the Americans "have a pious horror of consenting to any Thing, which may intail slavery on their Posterity," he continues immediately to explain that this horror has its source in the understanding of the value of liberty: "They think that the liberties of mankind and the glories of human nature is in their Keeping." Dickinson's lament that "we are become criminal in the sight of [the British] by refusing to be guilty of the highest crime against ourselves and our posterity" is not overblown rhetoric but a reflection of a strongly held and carefully thought out conviction that liberty is essential to humanity.[15] In that conviction lies the source of the American Revolution.

The Americans' focus on the British constitution as guarantor of liberty can be clearly seen through a consideration of the constitutional debate between the government in England and the colonists. Although the purpose of this book is to explain American arguments in response to British actions during the revolutionary period and not to explain in detail the events and arguments in Britain that gave rise to those actions, a brief study of British responses to colonial arguments can show the American position in sharper relief.

Although the controversy began with British attempts to tax the

15. L. H. Butterfield (ed.), *Diary and Autobiography of John Adams* (4 vols.; Cambridge, 1963), I, 282; *PWD*, I, 345.

colonists in order to secure additional revenue, it quickly grew, in Britain as in the colonies, into a controversy over a fundamentally important constitutional issue. However, the two parties were not concerned about the same constitutional issue. The colonial campaign against the Stamp Act featured the argument that Parliament did not have the authority to tax the Americans because the colonists were not represented therein. That campaign also established a colonial boycott on British goods, and it was the resulting pressure from British citizens that led to Parliament's repealing the act.[16] Far from accepting the American argument, however, the government in Britain saw a need to state explicitly and officially that the American claims about parliamentary authority were erroneous. Thus Parliament passed the Declaratory Act to assert its complete authority to legislate for the colonies. Thereafter, both for the colonists and for the government in London, the fundamental issue was to be found in the Declaratory Act.

From the point of view of the British Parliament, the key virtue of the British constitution was to be found in the principle of parliamentary supremacy over the Crown. This principle, an essential one for preventing arbitrary rule by the king, had been firmly established with the Glorious Revolution of 1688, less than one hundred years before the crisis between Great Britain and her American colonies. To the leadership in London, it was a principle not to be compromised or questioned in any way. According to commentators on the British empire, "The essence of the imperial claim was that Parliament's right to determine the limits of its own power was illimitable."[17] But in denying the authority of Parliament over them, the Americans had questioned this most basic principle of the constitution. The purpose of the Declaratory Act was to restate the jealously guarded position of parliamentary supremacy, a position from which the British government never wavered. Just as it did for the colonists, this constitutional issue grew in significance for the British during the revolutionary period to the point that by 1775 its attempt to defend the basis of the constitution was of "overriding" importance to the ministry.[18]

16. Edmund S. Morgan, *The Birth of the Republic, 1763–89* (Rev. ed.; Chicago, 1977), 28–32.

17. Tucker and Hendrickson, *First British Empire*, 179.

18. Richard W. Van Alstyne, *Empire and Independence* (New York, 1965), 63. For thorough discussions of this constitutional issue and its importance from the British perspective, see Van Alstyne; Randolph G. Adams, *Political Ideas of the American Revolution* (3rd ed.; New York, 1958); and Tucker and Hendrickson, *First British Empire*.

From a certain perspective the Americans were not insensitive to the constitutional problem raised by the British government. Yet, with the exception of James Otis, the colonists did not treat the need the British perceived for parliamentary supremacy as a fundamentally important constitutional issue. They wrestled with a managerial problem posed by their rejection of parliamentary supremacy but not with Parliament's principled concern.

The problem the colonists did address involved the management of the empire. The colonies and Great Britain were part of the same empire. They were subjects of the same king, and they were so because, according to Samuel Adams, John Adams, and Thomas Jefferson, the colonists had contracted with the Crown upon coming to America. The Americans insisted that this contract with the king in no way granted any authority to Parliament over them. Yet because the colonies were part of the same empire with Great Britain, most of the Americans realized that it was in the interest of all parts of the empire for there to be some final legislative authority on imperial matters affecting the common interest.

John Adams addresses this point with careful reasoning and detailed discussion of legal precedents in his "Novanglus" letters. There he demonstrates that while the colonists never granted the general authority to legislate for them to Parliament, they did consent to parliamentary regulation of trade. This consent to the regulation of trade was granted because of the need for a common trade policy in the British empire and because Parliament, "being the most powerful legislature in the dominions," was the logical body to establish that policy. Although he is less clear on how the authority came into being, John Dickinson too argues that "parliament unquestionably possesses a legal authority to *regulate* the trade of *Great-Britain*, and all her colonies." This authority, he continues, "is essential to the relation between a mother country and her colonies; and necessary for the common good of all. . . . We are but parts of a *whole*; and therefore there must exist a power somewhere to preside, and to preserve the connection in due order."[19] Only Thomas Jefferson rejected parliamentary authority to regulate trade.

By and large, then, the colonists did grant Parliament a supremacy but only in a particular area—that involving the trade relationships among the various component parts of the empire. This imperial supremacy was admitted, not pursuant to an argument about the

19. *JA*, IV, 111–12; *JD*, 312.

British constitution, but as the result of an argument about common imperial interests. In granting the authority to regulate trade, the colonists did not address the constitutional issue that led Parliament to pass the Declaratory Act. Parliament's insistence on its own supremacy was derived primarily, not from a concern for efficiency in imperial relationships, but from a fundamental principle established in the Glorious Revolution. The colonial admission of Parliament's authority to regulate trade did not address that fundamental principle and could not form the basis for an acceptable compromise with Parliament on the issue. From Parliament's perspective, the issue of parliamentary supremacy could not be resolved through compromise.

How did the colonists address the constitutional issue of the supremacy of Parliament? They addressed it by focusing on a part of the British constitution that they believed to be as fundamental and impossible to compromise as the British believed the principle of parliamentary supremacy to be. To the Americans, the relevant constitutional point was not about parliamentary supremacy; it was about liberty.

The American thinker for whom the issue was most troublesome was the first great intellectual leader of the revolutionary period, James Otis. Otis' difficulty arose from his conviction that the American colonists were Britons like those residing in England, whose government had been consented to in 1688. Unlike his American successors, Otis did not argue that the Americans, in leaving Great Britain, became free agents who made their own political arrangements thereafter. All political arrangements affecting the colonists were, for Otis, the same as those affecting all Britons. Thus he believed that Parliament was supreme because, as the British government argued throughout the revolutionary period, the Glorious Revolution had made it so.

Yet in discussing the British constitution as established through the Glorious Revolution, Otis considered not only the constitutional issue raised by the British throughout the period preceding the American Revolution but also the issue that was fundamental to the Americans. While it was true that the constitution made Parliament supreme, it was also most emphatically true that the constitution had as its basis certain fundamental principles of liberty, including the principle that *"the supreme power cannot take from any man any part of his property, without his consent in person or by representa-*

tion."[20] Thus Otis argued that although Parliament was supreme, the very thing that made it supreme also prohibited it from taxing the Americans because they were not represented in it.

When Henry, Dickinson, the Adamses, and Jefferson argued about the British constitution, they argued only about the principle of no taxation without representation. They saw that the fundamental principle of the British constitution was liberty: the Glorious Revolution had been about liberty and had established the constitution of which John Adams could say, "Liberty is its end, its use, its designation, drift, and scope."[21] For those residing in Great Britain, the means to protect this liberty belonging to human beings by nature and according to the British constitution was the prevention of absolute, arbitrary rule by establishing parliamentary supremacy, that is, by placing the supreme governmental power in the hands of the people's representatives. Thus parliamentary supremacy for the people living in Britain was not the fundamental principle of the constitution; it was merely the method used to implement the fundamental principle of the constitution. The same method of implementation could not work for the American colonists both because they had not consented to its use in their case and because they were not represented in Parliament.

At its deepest level—the level at which the Americans discussed it—the British constitution was not about parliamentary supremacy. It was about liberty. It was this point, and not the British point about the importance of the supremacy of Parliament over the king, that the colonists raised when they considered the constitution. In most instances, therefore, colonial arguments about the British constitution simply ignored the British arguments about that same constitution. For Thomas Jefferson, however, the discussion involved a direct attack on the principle of parliamentary supremacy over the Crown. When in *Summary View* Jefferson calls for the king to use his veto against Parliament to protect the colonists, he is asking the king to do something that was, to Parliament, unthinkable. "It would mean a repudiation of the Revolution of 1688, an outright challenge to the authority of Parliament, whose position the Revolution had firmly secured after a century of dissension and war with the Stuart kings."[22] From Jefferson's point of view, on the other hand, his proposal was

20. *JO*, 446.
21. *JA*, III, 479.
22. Van Alstyne, *Empire and Independence*, 56.

one designed to secure colonial liberty and hence to secure the victory of 1688.

There was one point in the constitutional dispute on which the Americans and the British agreed. They agreed that the Glorious Revolution had been against absolute, arbitrary governmental power. For the British, in overthrowing such power the Revolution of 1688 had established parliamentary supremacy; for the Americans, it had established the right of the people to consent to be governed. During the revolutionary period, both sides saw themselves as struggling to preserve the legacy of 1688—a legacy of such importance that neither side would compromise it. As one commentator has put it, to the Americans Parliament's victory over the Crown at the end of the seventeenth century was "a victory for the principle of legislative supremacy, but for the supremacy of their own legislatures, not that of Parliament, over the colonies." Or, in the words of another, "what the colonists had once claimed against prerogative they would now claim against Parliament."[23] The Americans thus saw themselves as the true defenders of the principles of the British constitution, and they made that argument by appealing to principles more basic and fundamental than the principle of parliamentary supremacy. To the colonists, if the Glorious Revolution was about anything, it was about establishing that the people's right to liberty was more important than governmental forms. Less than ninety years after 1688, the Americans would fight in defense of that same principle.

23. Merrill Jensen, "Commentary," in Adams, *Political Ideas*, 10; Tucker and Hendrickson, *First British Empire*, 163.

EIGHT

Liberty and Virtue

❧

In the course of making his argument about the goals sought by the American revolutionaries, Gordon Wood writes that "no phrase except 'liberty' was invoked more often by the Revolutionaries than 'the public good.'"[1] From this observation Wood moves to the conclusion that the public good, understood in classical and Christian terms, was the goal of the Revolution. The Americans, he argues, desired to use government to inculcate in the citizens the virtues of character sought in those traditions, to reach a public good "prior to and distinct from individual interests." The argument is a curious one, for having noted that "liberty" was the most frequently used term in the discourse of the revolutionary period, Wood attempts to argue that the colonists sought not liberty—a political goal that accentuates individual interests—but rather a goal that would involve educating people to believe they ought to deny themselves the satisfaction of their individual interests. However, as the American revolutionaries made clear in their writings, their first and most important goal was liberty. They believed liberty to be something of crucial importance; they believed it to be threatened by the actions of the government in London; and they acted to preserve it.

Nonetheless, although it is seriously—indeed fundamentally—misleading to argue that the Americans had it in mind to create a political regime whose primary purpose would be to use political action to create human excellence as understood in classical and Christian thought, it is true that the Americans of the revolutionary period often spoke of the importance of virtue as well as of the need

1. Gordon S. Wood, *The Creation of the American Republic, 1776–1787* (Chapel Hill, 1969), 55.

125

for citizens to seek the public good. Careful consideration of the colonists' arguments, however, leads to the realization that when they spoke of the public good, the Americans had in mind not something that was distinct from individual interests but rather something that was designed to make the pursuit of those interests easier. Similarly, when they spoke of virtue in the context of politics, the Americans most often did not have in mind classical or Christian excellence. Their notion of virtue could be tied directly to the need to create a government that would secure individual rights effectively.

That the colonists' understanding of the good to be sought by politics differed from the classical understanding can be shown initially by placing in context some of the phrases Wood quotes from the revolutionaries in drawing the opposite conclusion. One of Wood's sources is Thomas Paine: " 'The word *republic*,' said Thomas Paine, 'means the *public good*, or the good of the whole, in contradistinction to the despotic form, which makes the good of the sovereign, or of one man, the only object of government.' " Although this passage indicates that Paine believed government ought to pursue the public good, it does not make clear what Paine understood the public good to be. Fortunately, in a passage that Wood does not mention but that occurs on the very page from which he quotes, Paine defines the public good: "Public good is not a term opposed to the good of individuals; on the contrary it is the good of every individual collected. It is the good of all, because it is the good of everyone: for as the public body is every individual collected, so the public good is the collected good of those individuals." Paine's definition of the public good is squarely opposed to Wood's assertion that the "common interest was not . . . simply the sum or consensus of the particular interests that made up the community."[2]

In attempting to establish that the public good as the Americans understood it was distinct from and prior to individual interests, Wood writes about clashing interests: "[they] were not to be dignified by their incorporation into formal political theory, or into any serious discussion of what ought to be. In light of the assumption that the state was 'to be considered as one moral whole' these interests and parties were to be regarded as aberrations or perversions, indeed signs of sickness in the body politic." Wood's quotation from the *Result of the Convention of Delegates Holden at Ipswich in the County of Essex* that the state was "one moral whole" does not suffice to prove

2. *Ibid.*, 55–56, 58; Thomas Paine, *Dissertations on Government*, in Phillip S. Foner (ed.), *The Complete Writings of Thomas Paine* (New York, 1945), II, 372.

his point, for he fails to examine that document's discussion of the nature of the moral whole of which it speaks. The *Essex Result* is a useful source for discovering the American mind of the revolutionary period, for it is the report made by a convention whose purpose was to consider the form of government and constitution for the state of Massachusetts. Accordingly, it represents the considered opinion not of one man but of a convention of the leading citizens of Massachusetts. So the context of the phrase quoted by Wood carries some weight and deserves examination: "When men form themselves into society, and erect a body politic or State, they are considered as one moral whole, which is in possession of the supreme power of the State. This supreme power is composed of the powers of each individual collected together, and *voluntarily* parted with by him. No individual, in this case, parts with his unalienable rights, the supreme power therefore cannot controul them." The document continues with a discussion of the assignment of rights:

> Over the class of unalienable rights the supreme power hath no controul, and ought to be carefully defined and ascertained in a Bill of Rights, previous to the ratification of any constitution. The bill of rights should also contain the equivalency every man receives, as a consideration for the rights he has surrendered. This equivalent consists principally in the security of his person and property, and is also unassailable by the supreme power: for if the equivalent is taken back, those natural rights which were parted with to purchase it, return to the original proprietor, as nothing is more true, than that *Allegiance and protection are reciprocal.*[3]

The *Essex Result* here makes it unmistakably clear that the individual is prior to the community. Some individual rights are unalienable—under no conditions can they be considered to be renounced by their holder. Other rights are alienable, but the individual, the document states with emphasis, *voluntarily* chooses to give these powers to the state. He chooses to do so not to achieve some good that is independent of interest but to obtain security for his person and property. The individual makes a contract with the government: he will give it a clearly defined and limited amount of power that is naturally his, and in return it will provide him with security. As soon as the state stops protecting his person and property—it need not positively infringe upon his unalienable rights, it need only stop providing ade-

3. Wood, *Creation of the American Republic*, 58–59; *Result of the Convention of Delegates Holden at Ipswich in the County of Essex . . .* , in Theophilus Parsons, *Memoir of Theophilus Parsons* (Boston, 1859), 366–67 (emphasis in original).

quate protection—the individual recovers the powers he gave to the state and owes that state no more allegiance. Revolution becomes just when the government fails to protect individual rights. Wood's statement that individual interests were not incorporated into formal political theory cannot be reconciled with the source he uses to make that statement. For according to the *Essex Result*, individual rights are the beginning and the end of political theory.

This brief sampling of the sources Wood uses to argue that the Americans wanted a political community whose purpose was taken from classical and Christian thought indicates that exactly the opposite is the case: the end of politics embraced by the revolutionaries seems clearly to be the modern one of securing individual rights rather than the classical one of creating virtues of character.[4] This should hardly be surprising, for this view of the public good is the one taken by all of the major American thinkers of the revolutionary period examined herein.

Still it is the case that discussions of the importance of virtue occasionally come from the colonial leaders. In order to understand those discussions, it is best to start with the realization that it is not virtue but the security of liberty that is, for the Americans, the goal of political action. The revolutionaries' discussions of the need for virtue most frequently are arguments that the maintenance of liberty in a republic requires certain virtues in the citizenry. Most prominent in these discussions is Samuel Adams, the man who called for the "*Christian* Sparta" in Boston. Adams wanted Bostonians to share the moral virtues of the classical Greek and the Christian traditions because with those virtues they would be better equipped to maintain liberty in the community. Virtue is politically important for Adams since men "will be free no longer than while they remain virtuous."[5]

The need for virtue in the people if liberty is to be preserved was also voiced during the revolutionary period by John Dickinson. In the *Farmer's Letters* he writes that "some states have lost their liberty by *particular accidents:* But this calamity is generally owing to the *decay of virtue*." Dickinson's concern is for the effectiveness of the tactic of nonimportation of British goods for persuading the British to repeal the Townshend Acts. As Dickinson explains in a letter ad-

---

4. For a more complete analysis of Wood's argument and the sources he uses in making his argument, see Gary J. Schmitt and Robert H. Webking, "Revolutionaries, Antifederalists and Federalists: Comments on Gordon Wood's Understanding of the American Founding," *Political Science Reviewer*, IX (Fall, 1979), 195–229.

5. *SA*, IV, 238.

dressed to merchants, that tactic had been very effective in gaining repeal of the Stamp Act: "The Sufferings of all Ranks of People induced *them* to oppose it— Business was consequently at a Stand.— The civil Courts were shut, and you could sue no Man for the Recovery of a Debt—You were therefore *obliged* to sacrifice a very considerable Interest; and you determined to import no Goods from Great-Britain, until it was repealed.—This was *your* Virtue!—This *your* Resolution!—Your *Patriotism* and *private Interests* were so intimately connected, that you could not prostitute the one, without endangering the other."[6] With the Townshend Acts, however, the merchants' private interests were not so directly affected. It was not they but the consumers who would have to pay the taxes on paper, glass, and tea. It was in the merchants' short-term interest to continue to import and sell British goods because in so doing they could continue to make a profit. It is for this reason that Dickinson calls for virtue—the virtue to consider the public good involved in pressuring Parliament to repeal the Townshend Acts. He calls upon the merchants to sacrifice immediate profits in order to resist the Townshend Acts.

At first, the virtue that Dickinson calls for from the merchants may appear to be a genuine sacrifice of private interests to the public good. But as he makes clear, this virtue is really an enlightened self-interest:

> A *people* is travelling fast to destruction, when *individuals* consider *their* interests as distinct from *those of the public*. Such notions are fatal to their country, and to themselves. Yet how many are there, so *weak* and *sordid* as to *think* they perform *all the offices of life*, if they earnestly endeavor to increase their own *wealth*, *power*, and *credit*, without the least regard for the society under the protection of which they live; who, if they can make *an immediate profit to themselves*, by lending their assistance to those, whose projects plainly tend to the injury of their country, rejoice in their *dexterity*, and believe themselves entitled to the character of *able politicians*. Miserable men! Of whom it is hard to say, whether they ought to be most the objects of *pity* or *contempt*: But whose opinions are certainly as *detestable*, as their practices are *destructive*.[7]

Failure to participate in nonimportation would be fatal and destructive to the merchants as well as to the rest of the colonists because were the principle of parliamentary authority to tax the Americans to

6. *JD*, 397, 440–41.
7. *JD*, 397.

be established, everyone's liberty would be removed and everyone's private interests would be severely harmed. The problem Dickinson fears is not that the merchants will act from their self-interest, but that they will fail to understand their self-interest. Dickinson is not asking the merchants to deny their private interests in the name of a selfless public-spiritedness; he is asking them to realize that when it comes to the preservation of liberty, there is no conflict between public and private interests. Public-spiritedness in the preservation of liberty is essential for the long-term interest of each, for while it may require short-term sacrifices, as in the case of resistance to the Townshend Acts, it maintains in the long term the community's ability to protect the liberties of all.

This republican virtue of public-spiritedness, seen by Samuel Adams as essential to the maintenance of liberty in a republic and by John Dickinson as essential for preserving liberty against the threats to it from the British Parliament, then, is a means to be employed by each person to maintain a political community wherein each keeps the freedom to act in pursuit of his private interests. It is based upon self-interest—even if the self-interest be remote—and it is a means to the achievement of the public good. It is not the excellence of character that is the public good according to the classical and Christian traditions.

Most discussions of virtue in the writings of the revolutionary leaders have to do with the need to sacrifice short-term advantage in order to maintain the liberty that allows long-term advantage. It would be misleading, however, to say that the writings of the Americans demonstrate no concern about the classical and Christian moral virtues—virtues understood to be good in themselves, ends of human action rather than means to the security of liberty. The questions of the importance of traditional moral virtue and of the role politics ought to play in fostering it in the people are discussed most frequently, clearly, and thoughtfully in the writings of John Adams.

During the dispute that culminated in the Revolution, John Adams' arguments were like those made by the other major leaders of American resistance from James Otis to Thomas Jefferson. He argued that the British were failing to secure the individual rights of the American colonists. His arguments originated in the teaching of modern political philosophers that politics should concentrate on securing the natural rights of human beings rather than on teaching human beings the lofty virtues of the classical and Christian traditions. Yet there is another persistent strain in Adams' thought that appears to take the opposite path: at times he does argue the need for virtue. In the days before revolution, his argument about the need for virtue was similar to the argument of Samuel Adams and John Dickinson, that virtue—meaning a willingness to sacrifice short-term desires for the public good—is necessary for the maintenance of liberty. Adams, like his colleagues, fears "the *weak*, who never could be brought to think of the consequences of their actions, but would gratify their appetites if they could come at the means."[8]

There are, however, occasions, relatively rare, when Adams treats the production of virtue as the purpose of government rather than as a means to another purpose, that of securing individual rights. This presents a difficulty because the modern teaching that government exists to secure natural rights is based upon an explicit rejection of the ancients' argument that government's purpose is to make human beings virtuous. Neither the ancients nor the moderns argued that it was possible to achieve both the security of rights to life, liberty, and property and the loftier virtues. Governments must aim primarily at one or the other because the project of securing rights appeals to the selfish material and physical desires of human beings whereas the project of creating virtue demands that such desires be controlled.[9]

The difficulty appears with clarity in Adams' *Thoughts on Government*, a work that he wrote early in 1776 to offer suggestions on the organization of new governments in the colonies. There Adams begins by stating that "the happiness of society is the end of government." He continues: "All sober inquirers after truth, ancient and modern, pagan and Christian, have declared that the happiness of man, as well as his dignity, consists in virtue. Confucius, Zoroaster, Socrates, Mahomet, not to mention authorities really sacred, have agreed in this." Yet when Adams moves from this discussion of ends to a discussion of forms, he also moves from ancient authorities to modern ones. His second list is composed of "Sidney, Harrington, Locke, Milton, Nedham, Neville, Burnet, and Hoadly." Of these modern thinkers he writes, "The wretched condition of this country,

8. *JA*, IV, 90. See John R. Howe, Jr., *The Changing Political Thought of John Adams* (Princeton, 1966), 39–45.

9. For a good discussion of the impossibility of uniting ancient and modern political principles, as well as for an application of this discussion to the American regime, see Martin Diamond, "Ethics and Politics: The American Way," in Robert H. Horwitz (ed.), *The Moral Foundations of the American Republic* (Charlottesville, 1979), 39–72.

however, for ten or fifteen years past, has frequently reminded me of their principles and reasonings."[10] From there Adams goes on to outline a scheme of government, involving a popular assembly, a council, and an executive, without elaborating on the influence of ancient and modern principles on this scheme and without indicating an awareness of the tension between the two sets of principles.

Fortunately, the sketchy *Thoughts on Government* is not Adams' only work on political architecture. His understanding of why a certain form of government is best is elaborated at great length in his three-volume work, *A Defence of the Constitutions of Government of the United States*. That work was written in 1786 and 1787, a decade after the Revolution. Its purpose, however, was to discuss the principles behind the state constitutions written at the time of the Revolution. Gordon Wood writes that the *Defence* "was the only comprehensive description of American constitutionalism that the period produced."[11] In this work there is a thorough discussion of the ends and means of government, a study of which can give us an understanding of the relationship between virtue and rights, between ancient and modern political principles, in the thought of John Adams.

The *Defence* is an argument about forms of government. Adams' goal is to defend the form of government instituted after the Revolution by most of the constitutions in the American states against a criticism made by the French philosopher Turgot. In 1778 Turgot wrote that the American constitutions were each characterized by "an unreasonable imitation of the usages of England." His central criticism is that "instead of bringing all the authorities into one, that of the nation, they have established different bodies, a house of representatives, a council, a governor, because England has a house of commons, a house of lords, and a king."[12] The attempt to balance different governing authorities, Turgot continues, was necessary in England to control the strength of the monarchy. It is unnecessarily divisive, however, in a nation of equal men. Adams' work, written in response to Turgot but for both European and American audiences, is designed to demonstrate the usefulness of the creation of three governing authorities and the danger of uniting all governing power in a single democratic body.

Adams was, of course, aware of the similarity between the Ameri-

10. *JA*, IV, 193, 194.
11. Wood, *Creation of the American Republic*, 568.
12. *JA*, IV, 279.

can constitutions and the British form of government. His argument, however, is that the similarity arose not from a blind reverence of the former colonies for the mother country but from a careful understanding of the nature of human beings and their governments. He produced the *Defence*, he writes, "to lay before the public a specimen of that kind of reading and reasoning which produced the American constitutions." Adams is firm on the point that the American system is the product of reasoning and not prejudice: "The United States of America have exhibited, perhaps, the first example of governments erected on the simple principles of nature."[13]

Adams agrees with Turgot that government must be "founded on the natural authority of the people alone" and that its purpose must be to preserve the rights and liberties of the people. He disagrees with Turgot on the question of whether a single democratic assembly can secure those rights and liberties effectively. In his criticism of American institutions, Turgot writes of the inadequacy of the definition of liberty offered by many republican writers. Such writers were content to define liberty as the rule of law. Turgot's response is that it makes a difference for liberty whether the laws are just or unjust, that is, whether they secure or violate the rights of human beings. In answering Turgot, Adams leaps upon the Frenchman's observation. "I shall cheerfully agree," he writes, "with M. Turgot, that it is very possible that laws, and even equal laws, made by common consent, may deprive the minority of the citizens of their rights." The great problem, then, is to find a system of government that will recognize at the same time the people's claim to political authority and the need to ensure that governmental power is used by the people and their officers for "protecting the lives, liberties, and properties of the people."[14]

The overall argument of the *Defence* is that this objective can be reached only if there are three institutions dividing the governing authority: a house of commons, a senate, and a separate executive. This political arrangement involves the use of "the only three discoveries in the constitution of a free government, since the institution of Lycurgus," which three are "representations, instead of collections, of the people; a total separation of the executive from the legislative power, and of the judicial from both; and a balance in the legislature, by three independent, equal branches." Even these great improve-

13. *JA*, IV, 293–94, 292.
14. *JA*, IV, 293, 278, 402, 557.

ments, the only progress in the science of politics in two or three thousand years, Adams writes, have not been frequently employed in the making of governments. Apart from the Americans, only the British have seen the importance of these discoveries. It is this British insight, and not mere American prejudice, that makes the British constitution, in theory at least, "the most stupendous fabric of human invention."[15]

The specific ends that Adams has in view for government are more clearly understood through a discussion of these modern forms. His argument is that government must be made up of three parts: a house of commons, a senate, and an executive. These three parts represent different parties made up of different natural orders of human beings present in any community. The commons represents the many, and the senate represents the few superior, the aristocracy. It is difficult to characterize the executive, for although Adams says that the executive represents the natural party of the one, he does not make clear what that natural order is in communities without hereditary monarchs. Adams' argument concerns the few and the many, who form interest groups whose desires and rights must be taken into account by government. He does not discuss the one—the executive—in the same depth or as an interest like the other two that must be addressed for reasons of justice and stability. His discussion of the executive is of a part of government whose importance lies primarily in its being a third power, capable of preventing either the few or the many from dominating.[16]

The democratic branch of the legislature is simply essential in a free government. If the end of government is, as Adams quotes from Marchmont Nedham, "the good and ease of the people, in a secure enjoyment of their rights, without oppression," it seems essential that the people have at least some share in governmental power. Americans know, writes Adams, "that popular elections of one essential branch of the legislature, frequently repeated, are the only possible means of forming a free constitution, or of preserving the government of laws from the domination of men, or of preserving their lives, liberties, or properties in security." Of these rights to life, liberty, and property, Adams treats property as the most important throughout the *Defence*. It should be noted, however, that for Adams, as for the other American revolutionaries, the security of property is

15. *JA*, IV, 284, 358.
16. *JA*, IV, 385. See John Paynter, "John Adams: On the Principles of a Political Science," *Political Science Reviewer*, VI (Fall, 1976), 65–68.

intimately related to the security of life and liberty. He writes that the word *republic* originally "signified a government, in which the property of the public, or people, and of every one of them, was secured and protected by law." From this meaning he draws a conclusion: "This idea, indeed, implies liberty; because property cannot be secure unless the man be at liberty to acquire, use, or part with it, at his discretion, and unless he have his personal liberty of life and limb, motion and rest, for that purpose." Adams argues that in order for the people to secure their liberties and property from oppression, they must use their natural authority to create a government that, in addition to establishing a popular branch, gives power to the few and to the one. He demonstrates through argument and many examples that "it may be laid down as a universal maxim that any government"—including, perhaps especially, a democratic one—"that has not three independent branches in its legislature will soon become an absolute monarchy; or an arrogant nobility."[17]

In order to understand the need for a branch of the legislature that represents the few, it is necessary to be precise as to what Adams means by the few. He is not primarily concerned about using the wisdom and virtue of the few best. While he agrees that there usually is more wisdom brought to bear on decision making in aristocracies than in democracies, and while he argues that it would be best to try to make use of the positive qualities of the few best in government, it is not the few best he has in view when he speaks of the natural order of the few. The group with which Adams is concerned can be identified by our examining the distinction he makes between "principles of authority" and "principles of power." The principles of authority are qualities that ought to be the qualities sought in office holders. They include "virtues of the mind and heart, such as wisdom, prudence, courage, patience, temperance, justice &c." These virtues ought to translate into power, but most often they do not. The qualities that are likely to belong to possessors of power—the principles of power—are "the goods of fortune, such as riches, extraction, knowledge, and reputation." Adams includes knowledge, "which is by no means necessarily connected with wisdom or virtue," because it comes from education and travel, which are usually more available to those of wealth and good birth. He further discriminates between the principles of power by noting that "riches will hold the first place, in civilized societies, at least, among the principles of power."[18]

17. *JA*, VI, 65, IV, 466, V, 454, IV, 371.
18. *JA*, IV, 295, 427.

Thus, the superior few in most societies will be defined by wealth more than by any other quality, in particular, more than by virtue, the real quality that divides the naturally superior from the naturally inferior. The interest of the few to be represented in the senate, then, is the interest of the wealthy.

Adams' decision to consider only conventional superiorities, not natural ones, when discussing political representation indicates his fundamental choice to adopt modern political principles and to reject ancient ones. The ancients' understanding of mixed government assumed an order in nature that humans should act in accordance with. It was understood to be critically important, for that reason, to secure wise rulers who might discern that natural order and use political power effectively to teach people to live well. Despite the claim that only rule by the wise or virtuous is just, the ancients might establish a mixed regime in order to quiet those who would seek political power for selfish reasons or to cope with the problem of not having enough virtuous people to rule. In any case, the ancient mixed regime is a form designed to bring as much virtue to bear on political rule as possible under given circumstances.[19] Adams' mixture, unlike the ancients', is meant not to secure the rule of wisdom but merely to prevent selfish groups from being able to use the power of politics to harm one another's rights. At the same time that his "principles of authority" are replaced by his "principles of power" as the qualities to be taken into account in mixing government, the ancients' fundamental concern to secure virtuous rulers is rejected.

Adams presents two results, both disastrous for the people's rights, that could follow from failing to supplement the democratic branch of the legislature with a senate to represent the wealthy. The first possibility is that the wealthy, deprived of their own branch of government, will make the people's branch their own. The common people have less money, less time to be concerned with politics, and fewer political arts than the rich. The people's disinclination to spend time on politics puts the wealthy, who are well known and visible, at a clear advantage in elections. This advantage can be further cultivated by the rich through the use of well-developed political arts, which can include the use of wealth to corrupt the people in order to win elections. Adams writes that if the wealthy "found an opposition among their constituents to their elections [they] would immediately

19. For a discussion of this sort of ancient political argument, see Harry V. Jaffa, "Aristotle," in Leo Strauss and Joseph Cropsey (eds.), *History of Political Philosophy* (Chicago, 1963), esp. 94–125.

have recourse to entertainments, secret intrigues, and every popular art, and even to bribes, to increase their parties." Since the merits of candidates in elections tend to be similar and since, therefore, the conscientious citizens' votes will tend to be divided fairly equally in most elections, the balance of electoral power tends to be held by "the most profligate and unprincipled, who will sell or give away their votes for other considerations than wisdom or virtue." The end result is that "he who has the deepest purse, or the fewest scruples about using it, will generally prevail."[20]

Adams' argument, then, is that he who moves from the premise that the people are the best protectors of their own liberty to the conclusion that legislative power ought to be contained in a single democratic assembly fails to understand that the people are unlikely to maintain control of that assembly. Instead, the few rich are likely to turn that seemingly democratic government into an oligarchy. Once rule by the people has become in fact rule by the rich, the government is likely to degenerate still further. The rich will form factions. The struggles between factions will eventuate in civil war. The civil war will end in tyranny. The people are more likely to keep their power, and therewith the security of their rights, if they give to the rich a part of the legislative power that will belong exclusively to the rich. "The rich, the well-born, and the able, acquire an influence among the people that will soon be too much for simple honesty and plain sense, in a house of representatives. The most illustrious of them must, therefore, be separated from the mass, and placed by themselves in a senate: this is, to all honest and useful intents, an ostracism."[21] The rich will be less likely to seek control of the people's branch if they have their own legislative branch to protect their property and satisfy their ambition. By this method, the people's branch, so essential for the preservation of liberty, is maintained as the people's branch.

Even if the people should maintain their power in a single legislative assembly, it is safe to say, Adams argues, that they would not use that power to secure individual rights. In the third volume of the *Defence*, he writes: "We may appeal to every page of history we have hitherto turned over for proofs irrefragable, that the people, when they have been unchecked, have been as unjust, tyrannical, brutal, barbarous, and cruel, as any king or senate possessed of uncontrollable power. The majority has eternally, and without one exception,

20. *JA*, IV, 308, V, 457, IV, 292, 444.
21. *JA*, VI, 59, IV, 406, 290.

usurped over the rights of the minority." Specifically, a legislature made up of a single popular assembly could not be expected to pay the "sacred regard to property" that it ought to pay. "Property is surely a right of mankind as well as liberty." From moral or religious motives, a popular assembly might restrain itself for a while from taking the property of the wealthy, "but the time would not be long before courage and enterprise would come, and pretexts be invented by degrees, to countenance the majority in dividing all the property among them" through abolition of debts and heavy taxes on the rich. The people, it seems, may be the safest repository of their own rights, but the majority is clearly not the safest repository of the rights of the minority. The rich minority "ought to have an effectual barrier in the constitution against being robbed, plundered and murdered, as well as the poor; and this can never be without an independent senate."[22]

If a government exists to secure individual rights, it must have a senate. But the need for a senate to represent the wealthy follows not only from considerations of justice to the rich minority. It follows also from a consideration of the well-being of all. Adams writes that once a poor majority has succeeded in its unjust redistribution of property and the precedent of redistribution is established, "there must be a perpetual succession of divisions and squanderings, until property became too precarious to be sought, and universal idleness and famine would end it."[23] An insecure right to private property would result not only in gross injustice to the rich but also in a worsened economic condition for all. Both justice and the self-interest of the people, then, suggest the establishment of a senate to represent the interests of the few rich.

There is in the *Defence* the same difficulty found in *Thoughts on Government*. Although the primary focus is upon the security of individual rights as the end of government, there are a few places where another goal appears. At one point, for example, Adams presents this formula for the purpose of government: "The end of government is the greatest happiness of the greatest number, saving at the same time the stipulated rights of all." This definition is made more specific when, two volumes later, Adams quotes with approval Aristotle's conclusion "that a happy life must arise from a course of virtue." Elsewhere, Adams writes that this virtue involves the classical virtues of "prudence, justice, temperance, and fortitude," but that its

22. *JA*, VI, 10, V, 152, VI, 8–9, 65.
23. *JA*, VI, 133.

most sublime form is Christian virtue, "which is summarily comprehended in universal benevolence."[24]

In the preface to the *Defence*, Adams writes that "whether the end
of man, in this stage of his existence, be enjoyment, or improvement,
or both, it can never be attained so well in a bad government as a good
one."[25] The statement is interesting for it suggests at once that there
is a distinction between the two goals and that Adams may be un-
decided as to which should be sought. It is possible for human beings
to find the greatest enjoyment in virtuous actions, and in such cases
there is no tension between enjoyment and improvement. But it is
not easy for most human beings to realize that the greatest enjoyment
lies in virtuous action; in most cases they are likely to define enjoyment in terms of physical and material pleasures only. This more
narrow definition of enjoyment is the one Adams has in mind when
he distinguishes enjoyment from improvement in terms of political
goals. The major argument of the *Defence*—the argument that government must be properly structured to secure individual rights—is
an argument that appeals primarily to the narrow human desire for
enjoyment. This is especially true of the right to property, whose
protection encourages most people to acquire the things that lead to
the satisfaction of material desires.

It is true that property can be used to support virtue rather than
simply to gratify appetites. Wealth is essential, for instance, for the
exercise of the virtues of liberality and magnanimity. But the security
of the right to property as a political goal is far different from the need
for property that arises when virtue is the political goal. Property in
and of itself does not create virtue, and people are far more likely to
seek to acquire property for reasons of material well-being than as
support for virtue when the primary goal of government is to secure
the right to property rather than to make people virtuous.

If the goal of enjoyment is present in Adams' dedication to the
security of rights, especially the right to property, the goal of improvement is present in Adams' statements that human happiness
consists in virtue—in performing one's duties to others and not in
supplementing one's own material well-being. Inspection of Adams'
argument in the *Defence* reveals that he did indeed understand there
to be a tension between enjoyment and improvement as ends of man,
as well as a corresponding tension between a government whose goal

24. *JA*, IV, 318, V, 458, VI, 206.
25. *JA*, IV, 294.

is to secure individual rights and a government whose goal is to create virtue in human beings. Inspection of the argument indicates further that while Adams himself believed that human happiness is found in virtue, he also believed that when the goals of securing rights and encouraging virtues conflict, government should choose to secure rights.

Part of Adams' concern for virtue is subordinate to his opinion that government ought to secure the rights of all. If government is to be just, then its officers must seek the common good rather than the satisfaction of narrow, selfish interests. Thus, if the right to property is to be secure, the majority must not rob the minority and the minority must not rob the majority. However, Adams counsels against the expectation that a desire to do what is good for one's fellows will restrain the unjust actions of governing bodies. Several times in the course of the *Defence*, he makes statements reminiscent of the caution in the fifteenth chapter of Machiavelli's *Prince*. "In the institution of government," writes Adams, "it must be remembered that, although reason ought always to govern individuals, it certainly never did since the Fall, and never will, till the Millenium, and human nature must be taken as it is, as it has been, and will be." And again: "To amuse and flatter the people with compliments of qualities that never existed in them, is not the duty nor the right of a philosopher or legislator; he must form a true idea and judgment of mankind, and adapt his institutions to facts, not compliments." The important fact about human nature, then, is not that men are sometimes capable of virtue but rather that the number of human beings who dependably act from virtuous motives is very small indeed.[26] Government is needed precisely because, left to themselves, people will violate one another's rights. It is thus foolish to expect genuine virtue to be useful in securing behavior for the common good. Such virtue it is simply too unusual to find and too difficult to create.

Whether virtue be considered as the end of human beings or as a means to the security of individual rights, the Americans have particular difficulties in creating that virtue. One problem stems from the size of the Americans' country. Adams notes Socrates' and Pythagoras' argument that politics would be oppressive "until mankind were habituated, by education and discipline, to regard the great duties of life, and to consider a reverence of themselves, and the esteem of their fellow-citizens, as the principal source of their enjoyment."

26. *JA*, VI, 115, 98–99, 8, 211.

Here Adams recognizes that the goals of virtue and enjoyment are not always incompatible, that virtuous acts can be seen as the greatest source of enjoyment. But he continues, saying that this alternative of educating people to virtue might be plausible in a small community but is utterly unrealistic for a large one. "The education of a great nation can never accomplish so great an end," so that in a large community it is unlikely in the extreme that people will identify enjoyment with virtue.[27] Thus Adams at once acknowledges and rejects the best political alternative. If government could create virtue, it would be good for both the community and its individuals. This alternative, however, is not available to a large nation; large communities cannot expect to create a virtuous citizenry.

The other special difficulty the Americans have in creating virtue in citizens comes directly from the goal of securing individual rights. John Adams realizes quite well that human beings who seek to acquire property are less likely to be virtuous than human beings who are not taught that they have a right to property. Toward the end of the *Defence*, he discusses Montesquieu's understanding of a republic, noting that for Montesquieu virtue is the spring of a republic. Adams correctly decides that Montesquieu has in mind neither Christian nor classical virtue but a kind of love of the republic that will lead to sacrifices of self-interest for the community. This love of the republic requires both a love of equality and a love of frugality, neither of which, Adams writes, is part of human nature. It is true that frugality is a virtue, but a passion for it "never existed in a nation, if it ever did in an individual." Adams suggests that republican virtue as discussed by Montesquieu may be nothing more than the absence of ambition and avarice caused by poverty. It is certainly true that for Montesquieu republican virtue requires that one be satisfied with poverty. Earlier in the *Defence* Adams noted the connection between poverty and virtue, but he argued that human beings would not choose to pay such a price for virtue.[28]

Of course, wealth in and of itself is not hostile to virtue. Aristotle argues that a certain amount of wealth is necessary for virtuous actions. Adams also argues that material luxury is an evil only in excess. The problem is not wealth itself but the dominance of the desire for wealth. When human beings become more concerned about improving their material well-being than about developing virtue, then the opportunity to pursue wealth becomes destructive rather than

27. *JA*, IV, 556–57.
28. *JA*, VI, 209, 207, 97.

supportive of virtue. Adams' argument is that given the opportunity, most human beings will live their lives in pursuit of wealth rather than virtue and that, therefore, if their lives are to be free from domination by the desire for material well-being, most human beings must live without luxury and without a realistic hope of attaining luxury. This poverty that can make virtue more easily attainable is especially unlikely in free states, for the love of wealth is so dominant in human beings that with the liberty to pursue riches, they will almost universally choose to pursue those riches. Adams writes that "to expect self-denial from men" who have the "power to gratify themselves, is to disbelieve all history and universal experience."[29]

Adams' argument that the opportunity to pursue material well-being will lead most human beings to live their lives in pursuit of material luxury is an argument made later by Alexis de Tocqueville in observing that most Americans are dominated by a taste for material well-being. Tocqueville writes of the existence of a "universal, natural, and instinctive human taste for comfort." He argues that this taste can be prevented from becoming the purpose of life if material well-being can be taken for granted (as it could be by the old aristocrats of Europe) or if material advance is impossible (as it was for the serfs of feudal Europe). But when material advance is possible and material position is insecure, people become very likely to live lives whose primary purpose is the pursuit of material well-being. Tocqueville writes: "If one tries to think what passion is most natural to men both stimulated and hemmed in by the obscurity of their birth and the mediocrity of their fortune, nothing seems to suit them better than the taste for comfort." Because this is the circumstance of most Americans, Tocqueville finds that "love of comfort has become the dominant national taste" and that "the main current of human passions running in that direction sweeps everything along with it."[30]

Adams and Tocqueville agree, then, that the freedom to pursue property makes it true that "a free people are the most addicted to luxury of any." The addiction, Adams writes, grew especially quickly in America: "In the late war, the Americans found an unusual quantity of money flow in upon them, and, without the least degree of prudence, foresight, consideration or measure, rushed headlong into a greater degree of luxury than ought to have crept in for a hundred years." But, he continues, though the war accelerated the growth of

29. *JA*, VI, 61.

30. Alexis de Tocqueville, *Democracy in America*, ed. J. P. Mayer, trans. George Lawrence (Garden City, 1969), 533–34.

luxury, the political principles of the Americans, together with their happy physical circumstances, made the growth of luxury inevitable. "In a country like America where the means and opportunities for luxury are so easy and so plenty, it would be madness not to expect it."[31] Only if the right to property were insecure would poverty grow in America, and only with virtually inescapable poverty would widespread genuine virtue be a realistic possibility.

Adams, then, understands that classical or Christian virtue on a large scale is unlikely in America because of human nature, the size of the American nation, and American political principles. He knows that the doctrine of individual rights exacts a toll in virtue. If politics encourages those rights, and especially the right to property, then the citizens will be less virtuous than they might otherwise be. Knowing this price, Adams argues that it is nonetheless more important for politics to secure individual rights than to encourage virtue. Moreover, Adams argues that those kinds of political communities that can succeed in producing virtue in their citizens are to be blamed precisely because they do so at the price of individual rights.

Not all luxury is evil. Adams writes that luxury in excess is evil and ought to be restrained by law and morality. The most effective restraint on luxury—poverty—however, allows no luxury at all. Poverty frustrates the natural desire of human beings to improve their condition.[32] Adams argues that human beings ought to be free to seek material ease even though this freedom will lead many to the evil of excess luxury. This point, as well as another justifying the choice to pay a price in virtue to secure liberty, is made in Adams' discussion of Sparta.

John Adams' discussion of ancient Sparta is especially interesting in the context of his cousin Samuel Adams' remark that he would have liked to see Boston established as "the *Christian* Sparta." The context in which the remark was made clearly indicates that Samuel Adams was referring to the need for virtue as a means to securing individual rights. But John Adams' discussion of Sparta suggests that his cousin was expecting too much from virtue in a regime dedicated to the security of individual rights. Moreover, while John Adams appreciates the accomplishment of ancient Sparta, he argues that it would be not only impractical but also wrong for the Americans to try to follow the Spartan example. He knows that Lycurgus' laws sought

31. *JA*, VI, 95, 96.
32. *JA*, VI, 95, IV, 520.

to shape character and succeeded so thoroughly that the Spartan regime enjoyed excellent longevity. Furthermore, he has mild praise for Lycurgus' system of "three orders and a balance." It was not perfect, writes Adams, but it was a system built along the right lines.[33]

Yet Adams' final judgment on the Spartan constitution is that it was "not only the least respectable, but the most detestable in all Greece." He is aware that in this assessment he differs with the "aristocratical philosophies, historians, and statesmen of antiquity." Indeed, it is Adams' acceptance of modern natural rights principles that leads to his strident criticism of Sparta. In particular, he criticizes the measures Lycurgus used to shape the character of the Spartans so as to make them concerned only with the public good. In order to create this attachment, Adams says, "it was necessary to extinguish every other appetite, passion, and affection in human nature." He objects to "the equal division of property; the banishment of gold and silver; the prohibition of travel and intercourse with strangers; the prohibition of arts, trades, and agriculture; the discouragement of literature; the public meals; the incessant warlike exercises; the doctrine that every citizen was the property of the state, and that parents should not educate their own children." That is, Adams criticizes the laws invading individual rights in the name of virtue. The Spartans' civil liberty, he concludes, "was little better than that of a man chained in a dungeon—a liberty to rest as he is." And it is in this context that Adams reminds his readers, with emphasis, that government "should never have any other end than the greatest happiness of the greatest number, *saving to all their rights*."[34] Clearly, then, when the things needed to secure rights conflict with the things needed to produce virtue, as they do with the right to property, Adams' choice is for rights.

There is more to Adams' condemnation of Sparta and his refusal to compromise individual liberty than the argument that human beings ought to be able to act to satisfy their natural desire for material well-being. He believes that the dignity of individual human beings can be realized only if they have the personal liberty to control their own actions. This point can be seen in a passage in which he objects to an argument Aristotle makes in the *Politics*. Adams quotes a summary of Aristotle's argument that since human felicity consists "in the operations of virtue, and chiefly in the exertions of wisdom and prudence," those whose occupations are not primarily concerned with

33. *JA*, IV, 542, 553.
34. *JA*, IV, 555, 553.

the exercise of those virtues, such as husbandmen, artisans, and merchants, ought not be allowed to be citizens.[35]

This "dogma of Aristotle," writes Adams, "is the most unphilosophical, the most inhuman and cruel that can be conceived." Although it is true, he continues, that farmers tend to be inattentive to public affairs, it is nonetheless necessary that they be allowed to participate in the election of the legislature if liberty is to have any meaning at all. Adams argues that so long as a man has "any small property, by which he may be supposed to have a judgment and will of his own," he must be allowed a role in government. Of Aristotle's argument he writes that "there is no doctrine, and no fact, which goes so far as this towards forfeiting to the human species the character of rational creatures."[36]

It is instructive to note that Adams appears to misinterpret Aristotle in this discussion. For Aristotle, it is precisely because human beings are rational creatures that the most reasonable ought to rule in political communities. More reasonable behavior will be required of all if the most reasonable rule than if all rule together. But for Adams what is more important is not that all people do reasonable things but that they have an opportunity to exercise reason, however imperfect it may be, in making public and private choices. For Adams, the observation that human beings are rational creatures leads to the conclusion that all human beings must be allowed to use reason in public affairs. He does not appear to comprehend Aristotle's argument that because human beings are rational creatures they ought to allow public affairs to be directed by the most reasonable among them in order that all may act in a more reasonable manner. Human beings cannot be human, according to Adams and the other American revolutionaries, without the opportunity to guide their wills by their rational faculties. A human being who always acts as he is told by a superior, no matter how good the laws or how much the actions correspond to the demands of virtue, is not really human. It is far more dignified for that person to rule himself and make frequent mistakes than for him to live a thoroughly virtuous life under command.

Adams argues that since human beings and nations are ordinarily actuated by passions and prejudices, it is foolish to expect tyranny to be prevented by the virtue of citizens and rulers. This is especially the case under free government, where human beings are more likely to

35. *JA,* V, 455.
36. *JA,* V, 457, 459, 456.

be moved by a desire for material well-being. Adams argues further that it is wrong for governments to take strong measures—such as those Lycurgus took—to stifle these narrowly selfish desires, for such measures would make it impossible for human beings to acquire luxury even in moderation and would also deny them the liberty and dignity appropriate to their humanity.

It is, therefore, most prudent to create a form of government under which self-interested human beings will be neither oppressive nor unjust toward one another despite their selfishness. This is the attraction, for Adams, of a mixed system that includes a popular branch, a senate, and a separate executive to hold the balance between them. When discussing the dangers to communities brought on by the desire for luxury, as well as the inevitability of the growth of luxury in the United States, Adams writes that "the problem ought to be, to find a form of government best calculated to prevent the bad effects and corruption of luxury, when, in the ordinary course of things, it must be expected to come in." The advantage of the mixed system is that it can prevent the bad effects of selfish desires from being realized. Even if the members of the three branches act for selfish purposes, the three branches "restrain each other mutually by the laws," so that oppression and injustice do not result.[37]

Paradoxically, having abandoned a dependence upon virtue to restrain tyranny in government, Adams insists that an advantage of his mixed government is that it is better than any simple form at producing virtue. To understand this argument it is necessary to recall the evils of unmixed aristocracies and democracies. In democracies the majority is led to "rob" the minority, and in aristocracies the few will oppress the many. Because mixed government places an effective check on both parties, neither will be able to commit its crimes. "Although the vices and follies of mankind, no more than their diseases and bodily infirmities, can never be wholly eradicated," Adams writes, "the balance of three branches appears to afford all that the constitution and course of things will admit."[38] While it does not positively encourage the formation of classical or Christian virtues, then, neither does the mixed system positively encourage vices. Herein lies the great advantage of the mixed and balanced system over others: it restrains the passions of men so that they can be satisfied only within boundaries that preserve the rights of all.

37. *JA*, VI, 94, V, 90.
38. *JA*, V, 289, VI, 182–83.

During the decade before the Revolution, Adams had been very disturbed about the system used to fill governmental positions in the British colonies. The best example is that of Thomas Hutchinson, lieutenant governor and then governor of Massachusetts. Not only did Hutchinson himself hold as many as four political offices simultaneously, but he also obtained governmental posts for his relatives. To Adams, the system rewarded, not skill and hard work, but family connections and political scheming. Edmund S. Morgan writes: "Adams' dedication to work was more and more affronted by the sight of men who had discovered a political shortcut to success and wealth. There was nothing more obnoxious to him than the man who satisfied his ambition and avarice by obtaining appointments from the crown." The system for which Adams argues in the *Defence* would not encourage the vices that are encouraged where offices are filled by corrupt means. Herein lies a major advantage of Adams' "trinity in unity": it curbs "the audacity of individuals and the turbulence of parties." It does so "by doing justice to all men on all occasions, to the minority as well as the majority; and by forcing all men, majority as well as minority, to be contented with it."[39] The failure to encourage men to develop those vices that lead to success under a corrupt system is perhaps the greatest encouragement to virtue, or rather lack of discouragement to virtue, that Adams' system provides. When the Americans called for virtue in the years leading to the Revolution this was one important problem they had in mind: how to establish a system of government in which office and policy would depend upon merit and argument rather than upon vice and corruption.[40]

Yet this is not all to be said in favor of the mixed system of government, for Adams claims that it does more to create virtue than simply restrain vicious behavior. Adams argues that his balanced government actually encourages certain patriotic virtues as well as certain bourgeois virtues. Here, though, it must be remembered that his analysis is comparative. He makes no claim that the system for which he argues makes human beings benevolent or selfless, but he does claim that it will make them act better than they would have acted under a system dominated by a faction of either the rich or the poor. The key reason for this is that the checks and balances in a

39. Edmund S. Morgan, *The Meaning of Independence* (Charlottesville, 1976), 13; *JA*, V, 316, VI, 152–53.

40. See *SA*, III, 236; and *JD*, 401.

mixed system allow neither the rich nor the poor to command, and these checks and balances make it more likely that the rewards of society will be distributed justly than it would be were either faction to have unchecked power. This just distribution of rewards, in turn, is likely to result in liberty and prosperity. Both the prosperity and the steady inability of the idle and vicious to gain financially from the system encourage frugality and industriousness. Furthermore, liberty, along with the desire for luxury, supports a desire for knowledge, especially knowledge that is likely to result in increased material well-being.[41]

Adams is not the only one among the intellectual leaders of the Revolution to argue that there is a connection between the security of liberty and the encouragement of the virtues of industriousness and frugality. John Dickinson makes the same argument in the *Farmer's Letters*:

> For as long as the *products* of our *labor*, and the *rewards* of our *care*, can properly be called *our own*, so long it will be worth our while to be *industrious* and *frugal*. But if when we plow—sow—reap—gather—and thresh—we find that we plow—reap—sow—gather—and thresh *for others*, whose PLEASURE is to be the SOLE LIMITATION *how much* they shall *take*, and *how much* they shall *leave*, WHY should we repeat the unprofitable toil? *Horses* and *Oxen* are content with *that portion of the fruits of their work*, which their *owners* assign them, in order to keep them strong enough to raise successive crops; but even *these beasts* will not submit to draw for their *Masters*, until they are *subdued* by *whips* and *goads*.[42]

Finally, there is Adams' argument that his mixed system can produce a kind of patriotism in the people. As the well-being of each person becomes more connected to the nation than to a party, which it will when no party is able to dominate the government, the "trinity" indeed becomes a "unity," and a "love of law, liberty, and country" becomes more likely than it would in a pure democracy or aristocracy. The sort of patriotism about which Adams speaks here is described by Tocqueville:

> There is another sort of patriotism more rational than [a simple feeling of love for country]; less generous, perhaps less ardent, but more creative and more lasting, it is engendered by enlightenment, grows by the aid of laws and the exercise of rights, and in the end becomes, in a sense,

41. *JA*, VI, 159, 90, V, 289.
42. *JD*, 401.

mingled with personal interest. A man understands the influence which his country's well-being has on his own; he knows the law allows him to contribute to the production of this well-being, and he takes an interest in his country's prosperity, first as a thing useful to him and then as something he has created.[43]

This patriotism, which is a love of country allied to self-interest, is the very feeling that Dickinson describes and seeks to encourage in arguing the importance of nonimportation as a means for securing the liberty of Americans against the assault presented by the Townshend Acts.

Adams makes no claim that the virtues encouraged under a mixed system will come to be the moving force behind the conduct of all, or even some, human beings. He argues only that their influence will be greater under a system where neither the many nor the few holds unchecked political power and where, therefore, both parties are forced to work together to govern than it will be under a system where either party holds absolute power. The purpose of such a system is to secure liberty, not to create virtuous behavior. Nonetheless, a system that secures liberty effectively is likely to encourage the possession of certain virtues.

There is a lack of clarity in John Adams' political writings stemming from his appreciation of the arguments made by both ancient and modern political philosophers. He agrees with the ancients and the Christians that human happiness is to be found in the possession of the lofty virtues of character. He believes, accordingly, that the goal of ancient politics was a worthy one because it involved bringing out the best in human nature. Adams also believes, however, that the means that would have to be used in any realistic attempt to reach that goal are unacceptable because they require severe restrictions on liberty. Such restrictions would involve the effective stifling of free will and, hence, would result in virtuous actions without a real choice for virtue. In removing freedom, they would actually destroy human nature rather than fulfill it. In the absence of spartan measures to remove the opportunity for vice, only education could make people choose virtue, and the vices of human beings are strong enough that only a fool would depend upon education's ability to make people choose virtue.

Since people cannot be expected, and should not be forced, to live as they ought, the course recommended by prudence, Adams be-

43. *JA*, V, 289; Tocqueville, *Democracy in America*, 235.

lieves, is to construct a political system whose primary purpose is merely to control the effects of narrowly selfish behavior and not to create human beings who will be genuinely virtuous. His system, accordingly, is based upon the belief that to preserve liberty is more important politically than to inculcate virtue. The disadvantages of a system with this goal are great: not only can it not be expected to initiate positive action to create in its citizens the "sublime" virtues Adams believes necessary to human happiness, but it also tends to discourage the formation of those virtues because it protects property and liberates people to indulge their natural desire for luxury, thereby encouraging human beings to pursue wealth. This profound disadvantage, however, is finally outweighed by a great practical advantage. A mixed system whose goal is to secure liberty is likely to result in less vice and injustice than would any realistic alternative. Liberty being as important as it is and human imperfections existing as they do, this imperfect political alternative is the best available because it does not discourage the formation of virtue in the way that more unjust regimes do. In the final analysis, although Adams' system tends to encourage the desire for luxury, it also secures liberty, and because it does so, writes Adams, the people living under it "may be happy if they will."[44]

The American Revolution was not undertaken with the goal of creating virtue in the citizens of the community. It was undertaken to secure the liberty of human beings to act as they might choose. It would be more accurate, then, to say that the goal of the Revolution was to secure people's right to be vicious than to say that its goal was to secure a public good as understood by the classical and Christian traditions. From the point of view of ancient political thought, the Americans would have to be seen as irresponsible for choosing not to use the power of politics for the purpose of creating moral virtue in the citizens. Indeed, Aristotle denied that an association whose purpose is as limited as that which the Americans set for themselves was even a political community. He wrote in the *Politics:*

> Any polis which is truly so called, and is not merely one in name, must devote itself to the end of encouraging goodness. Otherwise, a political association sinks into a mere alliance which only differs in space from other forms of alliance where the members live at a distance from one another. Otherwise, too, law becomes a mere covenant—or (in the phrase of the sophist Lycophron) 'a guarantor of men's rights against

one another'—instead of being, as it should be, a rule of life such as will make the members of a polis good and just.[45]

To the Americans, however, the purpose of law is to guarantee men's rights against one another, and it is the ancients who hold a defective view of politics. Their view is defective because while it is based upon the correct opinion that human beings ought to be virtuous, it is based upon too simple a notion of how they might be made virtuous. The ancients neglect the fact that human reason—the natural human ability to make choices—makes liberty natural to human beings. Without liberty, without making their own choices about how to live and act, human beings cannot be genuinely virtuous. Virtuous behavior, if demanded by government, is not genuinely virtuous and makes, not for an excellent human being, but for a subhuman creature that appears to act well but does not employ human faculties in acting well. Because liberty is essential to humanity, free choice is essential to human excellence.

This argument that genuine virtue requires of each the free use of his own reason creates a difficult political problem. The Americans realize that reason is required to be educated if it is to be used well. Education necessarily implies some restriction of freedom. It is education, the presence of developed reason, that makes the difference between liberty and license, a distinction the Americans were all very aware of and very anxious to maintain.[46] The difference between the Americans and the ancients is not that the ancients recognize the need for education to produce human excellence and the Americans do not. The difference is the Americans argue that education without liberty will not produce excellence. Accordingly, they put their emphasis upon the need for government to secure freedom. By demanding virtuous actions of the citizens, the Americans believe, government makes virtue impossible. By allowing freedom, on the other hand, government does the best that it can do to encourage virtue: it allows people to choose to act well. Adams argues that people in ancient Sparta could be neither excellent nor happy because they had no freedom to choose. Americans, on the other hand, because the government allows them the liberty inherent in their natures, "may be happy if they will."

The argument of this chapter is that the Americans did not have in mind as the goal of their revolution the creation of a political commu-

---

45. Ernest Barker (ed.), *The Politics of Aristotle* (London, 1946), 1280b, 119.
46. See, for example, *JA*, III, 462; *JD*, 406.

nity united by a view of the public good as expressed in the classical and Christian traditions. In making the argument we come full circle in a way. For although the Americans did not seek to use political power to make people virtuous and to establish the public good of the classical and Christian traditions, they did seek to use political power in the only way they believed it could be used if virtue was to be possible. Virtue was not the goal; liberty was. They believed that without liberty, virtue—human excellence—is impossible. The virtuous way to use political power, they believed, is to use it not to command good actions but to allow free choice. In struggling for liberty the colonists saw themselves as participating in an honorable battle—a battle where the stakes were nothing less than human dignity. When the signers of the Declaration of Independence call upon their sacred honor and when John Dickinson writes for the Continental Congress that "honour, justice, and humanity forbid us tamely to surrender that freedom which we received from our gallant ancestors and which our innocent posterity have a right to receive from us," they are registering their belief that virtuous human beings give themselves, their fellows citizens, and their posterity the dignity of being recognized as rational creatures capable of deciding for themselves how to act.[47]

47. *PWD*, II, 96.

NINE

Liberty and Political Prudence

꧁꧂

Were the American actions during the revolutionary period rational? Or were those actions determined by an ideology that led the colonists to expect to see a conspiracy behind every governmental action and so to overreact to measures taken by the government in Britain that in fact posed no serious threat to the political well-being of the Americans? Having listened "with care to what the Revolutionaries themselves said was the reason there was a revolution," as Bernard Bailyn correctly says we must do if we wish to understand the event, we are in a position to consider the question raised by Bailyn's analysis about the relative importance of irrational fears and rational calculation in leading the Americans to act as they did. We can judge which is more correct: Bailyn's understanding of the American revolutionaries as men who "were not striving to act reasonably or logically," or the revolutionaries' presentation of themselves in the Declaration of Independence as prudent, reasonable, and responsible statesmen.[1]

We can consider, as an initial indication, Bailyn's argument about Thomas Hutchinson, the most important and most hated loyalist. Hutchinson was, according to Bailyn, very much the victim of a revolutionary psychosis: "The distrust and animosity Thomas Hutchinson inspired surpass any ordinary bounds. The reactions he stirred are morbid, pathological, paranoiac in their intensity." Hutchinson is portrayed by Bailyn as an embattled official whose prudence and pragmatism were no match for the ideological frenzy

1. Bernard Bailyn, The Origins of American Politics (New York, 1968), 11; Bailyn, The Ordeal of Thomas Hutchinson (Cambridge, 1974), 380.

153

driving his adversaries. He was, in Bailyn's words, "defeated in the end" by "the incapacity of sheer logic, of reason, compelling in its own terms . . . to control or even fully to comprehend an upsurge of ideological passion."[2]

The most dramatic display of this ideological passion, according to Bailyn, was the ransacking of Hutchinson's home by a Boston mob protesting the passage of the Stamp Act. Bailyn describes this event in a way that leads his reader to conclude that only pathological behavior could account for the attack. After all, he notes, Hutchinson had not been appointed a stamp master. Moreover, Hutchinson had even stated his opposition to the act, albeit in private. What then but ideologically produced paranoia could explain a mob's turning on Hutchinson?

It could have been something other than ideology. When news reached the colonies that Parliament was on the verge of passing the Stamp Act, most colonies drew up petitions of protest. Almost all of these petitions protested the act's passage on the grounds that it was an unconstitutional violation of the colonists' rights. Massachusetts, however, was an exception. Massachusetts drafted a document that made no mention of the colonists' rights and, because it conceded that traditional colonial control over taxation was a matter of mere "favor" from Parliament, implicitly granted that the colonists did not have the sole right to tax themselves. It was Hutchinson who had drafted the Massachusetts petition. In addition, as head of the Council, he had for more than a week filibustered against all attempts by the assembly to pass a more strongly worded petition. He had, in effect, frustrated the public will. As the crowning insult, when the act was finally passed, it was Hutchinson's brother-in-law, Andrew Oliver, who became stamp master for the colony.

That the mob reacted as it did, then, is quite understandable. One need not follow Bailyn and reduce the colonists' animosity toward Hutchinson to the "morbid, pathological, [or] paranoiac" to comprehend their anger. After all, Hutchinson was a man who had, over a relatively short period, acquired and held simultaneously the posts of assemblyman, probate judge, president of the Council, lieutenant governor, and chief justice of the Massachusetts Supreme Court. Here was a man who, while he was lieutenant governor and governor, married off three of his children to the other leading family of the state, the Olivers, and who, upon assuming the office of governor,

2. Bailyn, *Ordeal*, 2, 75.

turned over the lieutenant governorship and his seat as chief justice to members of the same family. Finally, here was a man who, while governor, ended the established practice of having the colony pay the governor's salary, in effect making the governor independent of the assembly's power over the purse. For Bailyn to describe John Adams' and the others' anxiety over Hutchinson's deeds as "paranoiac" seems to suggest that Hutchinson was a good friend of colonial liberty. That was not the case.

Another indication that the interpretation of the Americans as simplistic ideologues is inadequate has to do with the length of the period leading to the Revolution. For ideologues, especially ideologues of a radical bent, the colonists were very slow in making the final break with England. Whether one dates the beginning of the move toward revolution with the passage of the writs of assistance in 1761, the Sugar Act in 1764, or the Stamp Act in 1765, more than a decade passed before the final break with the government in London occurred. Patrick Henry's claim in the Virginia Resolves that anyone who should maintain that Parliament had a right to tax the colonists "shall be deemed an Enemy to his Majesty's Colony" was enthusiastically received by his fellow citizens a full ten years before shots were fired on the common at Lexington.[3] As late as 1776, a good third of the colonies, especially the middle and southern colonies, were still seeking an accommodation with England. The desire not to break away from British rule was shared until the middle 1770s by the very men who were the intellectual and political leaders of American resistance. Radical Samuel Adams did not decide in favor of independence until 1775. John Adams and Thomas Jefferson decided that independence was inevitable in the same year.[4] John Dickinson was actually opposed to the Declaration of Independence, though no longer to the idea of independence, in 1776. This reluctance of the Americans to break finally with the mother country does not seem consistent with Bailyn's portrayal of them as inescapably bound to a particular radical ideology.

In fact, the reluctance of the Americans to declare themselves independent from the mother country had its source in the same desire for liberty that ultimately led them to revolution. The impor-

3. This phrase is from the seventh of the Virginia resolves. Although not passed by the House of Burgesses, this resolution was among those that newspapers in other colonies reported as having been passed and was therefore important in exciting resistance to the Stamp Act.

4. *JA*, IX, 416; *TJ*, I, 165.

tance of liberty had been felt and understood by the Americans long before the revolutionary crisis began. For years before the 1760s Americans had been taught about liberty, its value for human beings, and its relationship to politics. One commentator explains the Americans' situation in this way: "The Americans who debated the nature and foundation of their rights and privileges with the mother country after 1763 were for the most part not dealing with new ideas. What they were doing was reformulating and reiterating ideas which had been a part of their English heritage, and to which they had appealed over and over in the course of a century and a half of experience as colonists in the New World."[5]

In the decades preceding the revolutionary period, the education about liberty came less through the newspapers and more from the pulpit. Perhaps the most important of the preachers who helped the Americans to understand and maintain a dedication to liberty was Bostonian Jonathan Mayhew. During the 1760s Mayhew was an influential radical in Boston. However, his career in educating his fellow citizens began long before the revolutionary crisis. In 1750 Mayhew delivered a sermon entitled "A Discourse Concerning Unlimited Submission and Nonresistance to the *Higher Powers*" that was soon published. It was to this sermon—one not delivered during the period when Americans perceived serious and persistent threats to their liberty—that John Adams later referred those "who really wish to investigate the principles and feelings which produced the Revolution."[6]

The purpose of Mayhew's discourse was not to call people to political action—1750 was too early for people to be considering revolution. The immediate purpose was theological. The sermon was preached on the anniversary of the death of Charles I, a day that was sometimes used by Anglican ministers to condemn the killing of that king, to revive the doctrine of the divine right of kings, and to defend the argument that Scripture requires subjects to submit to absolute government. Although the doctrine of divine right had never been widely preached in the colonies, Mayhew was concerned that he had seen in a recent pronouncement of Boston's Anglicans a "strange sort of frenzy . . . preaching passive obedience, worshiping Charles I, and cursing the dissenters and puritans for murdering him."[7] The pros-

5. Merrill Jensen, "Commentary," in Randolph G. Adams, *Political Ideas of the American Revolution* (3rd ed.; New York, 1958), 6.

6. Charles W. Akers, *Called Unto Liberty* (Cambridge, 1962), 93.

7. Bernard Bailyn (ed.), *Pamphlets of the American Revolution, 1750–1776*, (Cambridge, 1965), 206.

pect of the Anglicans' preaching in favor of authoritarianism and against liberty prompted Mayhew to attempt to demonstrate that Scripture does not require unhesitating political submission. The conflict was thus immediately about theology but ultimately about an issue as directly political as the proper relationship between ruler and ruled.

The sermon is on a passage from Paul's Epistle to the Romans that begins with "let every soul be subject unto the higher powers" and includes the pronouncement that "whosoever therefore resisteth the power, resisteth the ordinance of God." Mayhew's objective is to show that the passage does not require citizens to obey government completely, regardless of the character of the government. He begins by explaining that Paul's statement was addressed to a group of Christians who were refusing all civil rule and then says that Paul exhorts the group to obey the magistrates because their rule contributes to the good of civil society as a whole. God supports civil rulers, thus, because their rule secures the common good. Mayhew tells his listeners the passage shows that "the true ground and reason of our obligation to be subject to the *higher powers* is the usefulness of magistracy (when properly exercised) to human society and its subserviency to the general welfare."[8]

The question implied by Mayhew's interpretation is whether obedience is required in all cases because in some or in most cases government promotes the general welfare, or whether obedience is required only when governments do what they are supposed to do but not when they undertake measures harmful to the common good. Mayhew argues that though Paul states the requirement of obedience in absolute terms, his purpose is merely to show the general duty to obey to people who believed that no obedience is required at all. Furthermore, it is clear from the passage that the rulers Paul describes are good rulers, not, Mayhew writes, "good in a *moral* or *religious* but only in a *political* sense; those who perform their duty so far as their office extends." A ruler, on the other hand, who does not exercise "a reasonable and just authority for the good of human society" is not given a scriptural claim to obedience.[9]

Mayhew carries the argument another step. Thus far he has indicated that Paul counsels obedience to good rulers because they benefit human society. The goal with divine support, according to this

8. Jonathan Mayhew, "Discourse Concerning Unlimited Submission and Non-resistance to the *Higher Powers*," in Bailyn (ed.), *Pamphlets*, 221.

9. *Ibid.*, 226.

interpretation, becomes the general welfare, and therefore it follows that God, who supports the good of society more than mere obedience, requires that subjects disobey bad rulers. Mayhew adds, in a footnote, that this duty to resist does not obtain when rulers fail to secure the public good in a few instances but only when rulers act habitually to ruin the subjects.

Mayhew claims the most plausible objection to his argument that the people have the right and duty to resist bad rulers—his argument applies to all forms of government, for any government may be good or bad, though it appears difficult for an absolute monarchy to be good—is that were the people to be told they have the right to resist, they would abuse that right. The result would be disastrous for good governments as well as bad, and the public good would be even less likely to be achieved since no government could be secure. Mayhew admits the difficulty of the problem but does not agree that the only available solution is a doctrine of unlimited submission. He suggests that though some wicked people will resist unjustly, the people as a whole could be expected to obey until they were "really oppressed to a great degree."[10] Making this point largely through the example of Charles I, Mayhew argues that the king had been viciously oppressive for many years before the people finally acted, legitimately, to remove his tyranny.

It is in Mayhew's treatment of the tyranny of Charles I that we find some treatment of the major remaining question. A teaching that God supports resistance to governments that harm the general welfare surely requires some discussion of what that divinely supported general welfare involves. Even in 1750, Mayhew seemed to be confident that his audience would have little difficulty in understanding the meaning of the public good to be sought through political action, and so there is in the sermon no sustained discussion of the question. What he took for granted the public good entailed is indicated in his statement that those who stood justly against Charles I made their stand "in defense of the natural and legal rights of the people against the unnatural and illegal encroachments of arbitrary power."[11] The public good, then, requires the security of the natural rights of individuals. More specifically, Mayhew mentions citizens' lives, consciences, and properties. Mayhew, thus, defines the goals of politics in the same way the colonists did in the 1760s and 1770s: the purpose of politics is to secure liberty.

10. *Ibid.*, 237.
11. *Ibid.*, 241. See also *Ibid.*, 238, 228, 222.

It is interesting to note the structure of the argument in Mayhew's sermon. He begins with a theological dispute: does the Bible allow resistance to civil rulers? His interpretation of the relevant scriptural passages leads him to conclude that God gives human beings the duty to resist rulers who harm the public good consistently. Mayhew then turns to the example of Charles I to show that the British subjects' removal of the tyrant was just. This last point turns upon an understanding that the public good consists in the security of natural rights and civil and religious liberties. Interestingly, when it comes to the application of the right to resist that Mayhew finds in the Bible, the relevant standard does not come from religion. In his discussion of the tyranny of Charles I, Mayhew does not turn to the Bible to define tyranny. He uses Scripture to maintain that men may resist governments that endanger the general welfare, but he derives his understanding of the general welfare not from the Bible but from modern political philosophy. It is Mayhew's discussion of the right and duty to resist in the name of liberty that John Adams found to be so descriptive of the principles and feelings that produced the Revolution.

Mayhew was by no means the first to make the critical connection between divine support for the public good and an essentially Lockean definition of that good, thereby teaching the colonists the political philosophy that eventually supported resistance to British rule. One of the first to make the connection was John Wise, an obscure Massachusetts pastor whose work was done in the second and third decades of the eighteenth century. Although he never cited John Locke, Wise argued that human beings' natural state is one of liberty and equality. Because liberty is insecure when each is the judge of what is necessary to preserve his own freedom, men leave this state of nature in order to preserve their liberties. They form a contract with one another, each giving up a part of his natural liberty to enable the community to govern itself. The civil society thereby created delegates some of its power to a government whose purpose is to secure individuals' natural rights: "The end of all government is to cultivate humanity and promote the happiness of all, and the good of every man in all his rights, his life, liberty, estate, honor, etc. without injury or abuse done to any."[12]

In the following decades, ministerial exposition of political arguments about the importance of liberty—arguments that would be

12. Clinton Rossiter, *Seedtime of the Republic* (New York, 1963), 223. See also Alice M. Baldwin, *The New England Clergy and the American Revolution* (New York, 1958), 28–29.

repeated and refined during the revolutionary crisis by the likes of Otis, Dickinson, and the Adamses—became more frequent. In 1744, for example, a Puritan minister published a pamphlet entitled *The Essential Rights and Liberties of Protestants*, in which he established a right to property not from the Bible but with an argument that is a clear paraphrase of Chapter Five of John Locke's *Second Treatise of Civil Government*:

> And altho' no one has originally a private domain exclusive of the rest of Mankind in the Earth or its Products, as they are considered in this their natural State; Yet since God has given these Things for the Use of Men and given them Reason also to make use thereof to the best Advantage of Life, there must be of Necessity a Means to appropriate them some Way or other before they can be of any Use to any Particular Person. And every Man having a Property in his own Person, the Labour of his Body and the Work of his Hands are properly his own, to which no one has a Right but himself; it will therefore follow that when he removes any Thing out of the State that Nature has provided and left it in, he has mixed his Labour with it and joined something to it that is his own, and thereby makes it his Property.[13]

The author follows this summary of Locke's theory of property with a summary of Locke's theory of the origin and purpose of government and civil society. Thus, in 1744 this minister was teaching the political principles that would later form the basis of arguments against British rule.

When these ministers taught the arguments of modern political philosophy before the 1760s, they were not contemplating resistance to British rule. Quite the opposite is true. When they argued, following Locke, that the purpose of government is to secure citizens' rights to life, liberty, and estate; that government should be limited so that it will not become a serious threat to the security of rights; and that limited government is established by contract, the ministers in the colonies were attempting to prove the British government was good and deserved obedience. They argued that the purpose of the British government was to secure rights, that the government was limited in power, and that both the rights and the limits were to be found in the British constitution and in the contracts that were constituted by the colonial charters.

This celebration of the British constitution as based upon the proper understanding of politics became especially fervent in the

13. Baldwin, *New England Clergy*, 66.

context of conflicts between the British and the French. Thus Mayhew, who in the 1760s was to become an important resistance leader, exclaims in 1754:

> And what horrid scene is this, which restless, roving fancy, or something of a higher nature, presents to me, and so chills my blood! Do I behold these territories of freedom, become the prey of arbitrary power? . . . Do I see the slaves of Lewis with their Indian allies, dispossessing the free-born subjects of King George, of the inheritance received from their forefathers, and purchased by them at the expense of their ease, their treasure, their blood!. . . Do I see a Protestant there, stealing a look at his bible, and being taking in the fact, punished like a felon! . . . Do I see all liberty, property, religion, happiness, changed, or rather transsubstantiated, into slavery, poverty, superstition, wretchedness!

During the Seven Years' War, the the era immediately preceding the revolutionary crisis, these arguments from the pulpit—that the purpose of government is to secure liberty and that the British government ought to be defended because it secures liberty—became stronger and more frequently delivered than ever. One commentator writes:

> It seems a most significant fact and one never sufficiently realized by historians that for the seven years before the beginning of the trouble with England the people had heard continually from the pulpit such ringing words upon the unspeakable value of their chartered privileges and their rights as Englishmen; of law and constitution as contrasted with tyranny and arbitrary government; of the danger of becoming slaves and losing all their freedom, civil and religious, under such a government; of the justification of war in defense of their cherished rights and liberties. The English constitution was to be defended at any cost because it assured a government of law, because it was so nicely balanced, each part with its own carefully defined rights and limitations, because it guarded so jealously the natural and legal rights of the subject.[14]

The Americans' education about liberty in the years before the 1760s, then, taught them not only that it was important for a government to be organized to secure liberty but also that they were ruled by the government in the world that was best suited to do so. At the beginning of the revolutionary crisis, the Americans' love of British rule was as real and strong as their love of liberty—they were, in actuality, the same love. For that reason, the Americans were very

14. Baldwin, *New England Clergy*, 87, 88–89.

reluctant to consider revolution until the middle of the 1770s, when it became clear to them that they would have to choose between having liberty and being Britons. At the beginning of the disputes between the colonies and Great Britain, the colonists were not disposed to find everything wrong with government; they were disposed rather to celebrate the accomplishments of British government in securing human liberty. James Otis states well the opinion of his fellow citizens:

> A continuation of the same liberties that have been enjoyed by the colonists since the [Glorious] Revolution, and the same moderation of government exercised towards them will bind them in perpetual lawful and willing subjection, obedience, and love to Great Britain: she and her colonies will both prosper and flourish. The monarchy will remain in sound health and full vigour at that blessed period when the proud arbitrary tyrants of the continent shall either unite in the deliverance of the human race or resign their crowns. Rescued human nature must and will be from the general slavery that has so long triumphed over the species. Great Britain has done much towards it: what a glory will it be for her to complete the work throughout the world!

Samuel Adams, writing to the Governor of Massachusetts for the Massachusetts House of Representatives in 1765, also expresses the respect of the Americans for British rule: "We inherit from our ancestors the highest relish for civil liberty; but we hope never to see the time when it shall be expedient to countenance any methods for its preservation but such as are legal and regular. When our sacred rights are infringed, we feel the grievance, but we understand the nature of our happy constitution too well, and entertain too high an opinion of the virtue and Justice of the supreme legislature, to encourage any means of redressing it, but what are justifiable by the constitution."[15]

This love of British rule that arose from the conviction that British rule secured the liberty of the citizens is also indicated by the changes in the arguments made by the colonists over the years leading to revolution. Although every major American intellectual leader of the period from James Otis to Thomas Jefferson made the connection between natural rights and the rights of British citizens, in the early years of the crisis colonial protests against parliamentary taxation were much more likely to depend upon arguments about the liberty guaranteed by the British constitution than upon arguments about the liberty that belongs to human beings according to nature. Patrick

15. *JO*, 459; *SA*, I, 21.

Henry's Virginia Resolves, for example, make a claim that the Stamp Act violates colonial rights, but rights as established by the British constitution and as belonging to the Americans through their citizenship and charters. The resolves do not make an argument about natural rights. In the early years of opposition, Samuel Adams also concentrated upon the rights of the colonists as British subjects much more than upon their rights as human beings.

The shift from an early concentration upon British rights to a later one upon natural rights is most clearly indicated by the language of the declarations issued by the various assemblies at which all, or nearly all, of the colonies were represented: "The Resolutions of the Stamp Act Congress" in 1765, "The Declarations and Resolves of the First Continental Congress" in 1774, and the Declaration of Independence in 1776. The first document speaks only of "the inherent Rights and Liberties of his [majesty's] natural born subjects within the kingdom of Great Britain." The second speaks of both "the laws of nature" and "the principles of the English constitution." The declaration speaks only of the "inalienable rights" with which human beings are "endowed by their creator." Thus the Americans began their debate with Great Britain on a rather "low legalistic level, finding it convenient to debate within the framework of the imperial constitution and the common law; but they gradually and inevitably climbed the ladder of abstraction until, by mid-1776, they were thinking and talking in the arid heights of natural law."[16]

At first glance it might appear that this shift from arguing about British rights to arguing about natural rights merely confirms the Progressive view that the revolutionaries were willing to change their arguments whenever it suited their needs. And it is true that the revolutionaries were willing to change their arguments to suit their needs but only because, as the crisis developed, the colonists came to perceive their needs differently. As long as there was a possibility that the dispute between London and the colonies could be resolved, still maintaining the liberties of the Americans under British rule, there was no need to raise the level of debate beyond the question of the things required by the British constitution. People do not think of rejecting a government that they believe to be the best in human history when that government makes a mistake. They merely seek to correct the mistake. It was only as the colonists saw more and more

16. *JD*, 184; Daniel J. Boorstin, *The Genius of American Politics* (Chicago, 1943), 77.

clearly that the violations of liberty by the British government would continue that the American rhetoric changed to emphasize the colonists' rights as human beings and not merely as citizens.

It would be misleading, then, to characterize the shift in the grounds of the colonial arguments as disingenuous or inconsistent. The shift demonstrates the colonists' strong intellectual and emotional attachment to the British constitution based on their understanding that the constitution embodied their natural rights. Their emphasis moved from British rights to natural rights only as they became convinced that their confidence in the British government's dedication to the security of their liberty was misplaced. In fact, as the colonists began to argue less about the rights of Britons and more about the rights of human beings, they were not changing the substance of their arguments so much as exposing the true ground of their original claims. Their principles did not change, but their prudence led them to apply those principles differently as circumstances changed. The Americans' understanding of the importance of liberty led them to support British rule at the beginning of the revolutionary crisis and to oppose it at the end.

Was it reasonable for the colonists to conclude that there was a serious threat to their liberty that required them to renounce their love for British rule? Was the threat real and as dangerous as they claimed, or were they overreacting? Did an irrational fear of conspiracy become so great in the decade before revolution that the Americans made insignificant and unconnected events into a great crisis involving a conspiracy to enslave them when in fact there was no conspiracy to remove their liberties?

Of course there was much talk among the Americans, especially as the years approached 1776, of the existence of a conspiracy on the part of certain British governing officials to remove colonial liberties. John Adams wrote of conspiracy in the "Novanglus" letters. Samuel Adams wrote in 1771 to Arthur Lee that he had "long thought that a Design has been on foot to render ineffectual the Democratical part of this Government." Five months later he wrote that "it seems by some *later ministerial mandates* and measures, as if there was a design to deprive us of our Charter-Rights *by degrees.*" In 1773 he wrote in a petition to the king that "there has long been a Combination of evil Men in this province, who have contemplated Measures and formed a Plan, to raise their own Fortunes and advance themselves . . . to the annihilating of the Rights & Liberties of the American Colonies." And Thomas Jefferson wrote in *Summary View* of a "deliberate, systematical plan of reducing us to slavery."[17] The question that remains, however, is whether the fear of conspiracy expressed by these colonial leaders was, given the events of the time, a prudent one or an irrational one spawned by a predisposition to see dangerous conspiracy even where there was none.

It is helpful at this point to recall the language of the Declaration of Independence. It says that the right or duty to revolt arises, not for light and transient causes, "but when a long train of abuses and usurpations, pursuing invariably the same Object evinces a design to reduce them under absolute Despotism." From 1764 to 1774 the Americans did not experience anything approaching the worst that despots can do. There was no large scale taking of private property by the British. In fact, most of the controversial taxes were repealed. There was no torture. There were no new and harsh restrictions on speech and the press, no attempts to restrict communication between groups. On the contrary, the press was allowed to spread its message of resistance, and the revolutionary leaders were allowed to express themselves freely, widely, and clearly to their fellow citizens. It does not appear, at least before the Coercive Acts of 1774, that the tyranny spoken of by the leaders of the American resistance was a tangible factor in day-to-day life.

If ordinary life in the colonies was not much different in 1773 from what it had been in 1763, why the change in the American disposition toward British rule? Why the fears of conspiracy? The answer is clear: the Stamp Act, the Declaratory Act, the Quartering Act, the suspension of the New York legislature, the Townshend Acts, the Tea Act, the payment of the salaries of colonial judges and governors by the government in London, and the stationing of large numbers of British soldiers in the colonies. The British Parliament, with the cooperation of the king, passed a series of laws that took away, or threatened to take away, the Americans' control of their own properties and governments. That is to say, the Parliament passed several pieces of legislation that denied colonial liberty.

In 1775 Edmund Burke explained to the British Parliament that one cause of the actions of the Americans was the colonists' understanding, especially the understanding that came from their education in the law. He describes it in this way: "This study renders men acute, inquisitive, dexterous, prompt in attack, ready in defence, full of resources. In other countries, the people, more simple and of a less

17. *SA*, II, 165, 225, III, 46–47; *TJ*, I, 125.

mercurial cast, judge of an ill principle in government only by an actual grievance; here they anticipate the evil and judge of the pressure of the grievance by the badness of the principle. They augur misgovernment at a distance, and snuff the approach of tyranny in every tainted breeze."[18] It was the consequences from the principles behind the actions of the British government that the American intellectual leaders found most threatening. Those principles, they realized, raised the prospect that future denials of liberty would be far greater than the actual denials of liberty they experienced during the period preceding the Revolution.

Following the understanding that the principles of a government may be more threatening than the first actions a government takes in carrying out those principles, the Declaration of Independence does not claim that prudent men revolt when acts of despotism are felt; it claims that prudent men will revolt when the *design* of despotism becomes manifest. Reflection proves that this is indeed prudent counsel. For the more solidly established a system of tyranny becomes, the easier it is for tyrants to prevent the threats to their rule from growing into serious ones. The best chance to prevent tyranny occurs before the design is well established.

The Americans were very aware that the most effective way to fight tyranny is not to allow it to become established in the first place. John Adams and John Dickinson, both of whom explore the relationship between rationality and the desire for liberty in their writings, argue that tyranny depends for its success upon creating and maintaining an ignorance in the people to prevent them from understanding that there is a better condition for human beings than slavery. An established tyranny could create in the people the slavish habits that would make the tyranny more easily perpetuated. Thus Dickinson writes that "usurpations, which might have been successfully opposed at first, acquire strength by continuance," and ends one of the *Farmer's Letters* with the injunction to "oppose a disease at its beginning." John Adams also writes that it is of critical importance to "nip the shoots of arbitrary power in the bud."[19]

The Americans also knew that it was no easy task to combat tyranny in its design phase. Two things are required: an appreciation of the existence of the design, and a willingness to sacrifice in order to combat the danger before the hurt it could cause is actually felt. The

18. Edmund Burke, *Speeches and Letters on American Affairs* (New York, 1908), 95.

19. *JD*, 323; *JA*, IV, 43.

great effort of the intellectual leaders of the Americans during the revolutionary crisis was to explain to their fellow citizens that there were severe dangers to liberty and that they ought to sacrifice in order to defeat those threats.

Samuel Adams, John Adams, and John Dickinson all discuss the advantage that a government seeking to become tyrannical holds over its citizens: it knows it is seeking to become tyrannical while they do not know. Only an incompetent would-be tyrant would announce his plans to remove a people's liberty before he had successfully done so. The people are unlikely to believe the worst until the tyranny is well established because it is easier for human beings to be controlled by their feelings than by their reason. Hence, human beings are unlikely to appreciate the tryannical nature of an act until they feel the oppression.[20] This tendency not to act against actions stemming from dangerous political principles is compounded by the fact that it often requires the sacrifice of short-term comfort to act against a political principle whose danger will be realized only in the long run. It was not in the merchants' short-term economic interest, for example, to participate in the nonimportation of British goods in resistance to the Townshend Acts, and in order to obtain their participation the leaders of American resistance had to make very clear the long-term danger posed by the principle of parliamentary taxation.

The writings of the American leaders were designed to combat this problem of the unlikelihood of people acting against tyranny until the severity of tyranny is felt. The various authors attempt to make the issues clear to the reason of their fellow citizens and so to secure those citizens' informed support for actions to protect their liberties. The purpose of the *Farmer's Letters*, for example, is to present a carefully considered and carefully constructed argument to the citizens of the colonies that the Townshend Acts violate liberty and threaten to set a precedent for future, more oppressive, violations. The writings of Samuel Adams during the relatively quiet period at the beginning of the 1770s constantly try to convince Adams' fellow citizens of the long-range danger posed by the attempts to remove from the colonial assembly the authority to pay governors and judges. In both cases the authors worked at clarifying the actions of the government in London to the colonists in order to make clear to reason what could not have yet been felt: that seemingly minor ac-

20. See *SA*, III, 284; *JD*, 311.

tions of the British government posed serious threats to the Americans' freedom to control their own lives in the future. Dickinson, Adams, and the others had strong faith in the devotion of the Americans to liberty; the reaction to the Virginia Resolves had demonstrated the strength of the Americans' love of liberty. All they had to do was to appeal to the reason of their fellow citizens to show them that the various acts passed by the British during the period of the revolutionary crisis were, in fact, dangerous to liberty.

Time and again the American authors wrote of the need to respond quickly and certainly to acts that tended to destroy liberty lest the problem become greater and the solution—if solution were still possible—more radical. Dickinson warns in the *Farmer's Letters* that the problem of threats to American liberty from the British government must be met early before those threats accumulate to the point that violence will be the only recourse: "Oppressions and dissatisfactions being permitted to accumulate—*if ever* the governed throw off the load, *they will do more. A people does not reform with moderation.*" Samuel Adams puts the point this way: "If the liberties of America are ever compleatly ruined, of which in my opinion there is now the utmost danger, it will in all probability, be the consequence of a mistaken notion of *prudence,* which leads men to acquiesce in measures of the most destructive tendency for the sake of present ease."[21] The more accurate notion of prudence that informed the actions of the intellectual leaders of the Revolution enabled them to appreciate dangers to liberty and to act upon those dangers as they arose. There was a revolution because those dangers continued to arise despite the efforts of the colonists to prevent them.

But was it prudent to perceive a design on the part of the British to remove American liberty? It is certainly not clear that there was any well-organized conspiracy in London to enslave the colonists. It is clear, however, that the treatment of the colonists by the British government changed markedly after the Seven Years' War. One study concludes that the actions of the British government with respect to the colonies were designed to increase the power of the central government and decrease the independence of the colonies and that "this assumption of responsibility . . . represented a fundamental change in the imperial-colonial relationship." Another commentator states the point in these words:

> Over the past decade it has become modish to dismiss colonial fears of conspiracy as they developed between 1763 and 1776 as simple para-

21. *JD*, 387; *SA*, II, 287.

noia arising out of a particular culturally conditioned mind set. But insofar as it implies that there was no real substance to these fears, such an interpretation is seriously deficient. Clearly the kind of conspiracy many colonists thought existed did not: there was no secret combination of power-hungry ministers seeking to destroy liberty in America. Since 1748, however, there had been an unmistakable and continuing effort by imperial authorities to bring the colonies under tighter regulation. . . . Given the colonists' customary expectations about the nature of the imperial-colonial relationship, this effort, and its many specific components, seemed to the colonists—and *was in fact*—a fundamental attack upon the extant moral order within the empire as they conceived of that order.[22]

Whether these British actions with regard to the American colonies after the Seven Years' War were designed to remove American liberty; whether they were even designed taking American liberty into account; whether they were the result of careful planning; whether the individual actions had enough coherence that they could be said to have emanated from a genuine policy; whether they sprung from a calculating desire for power, from a shortsighted desire to improve the rule of the empire, from ignorance, or from incompetence—these were questions that, by 1776, it would have been irresponsible for the American statesmen to entertain. The fact that had to control their thinking by then was that for a period of more than a decade the British government had undertaken action after action resulting in the restriction of American liberty. There were acts taxing the Americans without their consent, acts restricting trial by jury, acts diminishing popular control of governments, and there was the stationing of large numbers of soldiers in the colonies. Whenever one act dangerous to liberty had been repealed, it had been soon replaced by another. Perhaps the most significant of all the acts had come early in the crisis: the Declaratory Act, which simply said that the British Parliament, over which the Americans had no control whatever, could do whatever it wanted to do to the Americans. It said that the Americans had no legal right to control their own lives. It said that in theory the colonists were the slaves of Great Britain. And as if the point had not been made clearly enough by the words of the Declaratory Act itself, that act was followed by the Quartering Act, the Townshend Acts, the suspension of the New York legislature, the

22. Robert W. Tucker and David C. Hendrickson, *The Fall of the First British Empire* (Baltimore, 1982), 86; Jack P. Greene, "An Uneasy Connection: An Analysis of the Preconditions of the American Revolution," in Stephen G. Kurtz and James H. Hutson (eds.), *Essays on the American Revolution* (Chapel Hill, 1973), 79.

stationing of more soldiers in the colonies, the British assumption of the authority to pay colonial judges and governors, the Tea Act, and the Coercive Acts.

In this context, only a shortsighted fool would have felt that American liberty was safe. Such a fool might have assumed a lack of desire to violate American liberty on the part of the British government. A prudent statesman could never have made that assumption in the light of those political circumstances. Thomas Jefferson is well aware of circumstances when he asserts in the *Summary View* the existence of a plan to reduce the Americans to slavery: "Single acts of tyranny may be ascribed to the accidental opinion of a day: but a series of oppressions, begun at a distinguished period, and pursued unalterably thro' every change of ministers, too plainly prove a deliberate, systematical plan of reducing us to slavery."[23] Jefferson's perception of a "systematical plan" is not the result of his being possessed by an ideology that leads him to see conspiracy behind every governmental action. It is the result of his rational analysis of the political events of the day. If there was no such plan and if, for that reason, there was irrationality contributing to Jefferson's conclusion that there was a plan, that irrationality was not in Jefferson but in London.

It is interesting to note that the speech that includes perhaps the most famous exclamation from an American during the revolutionary crisis contains as its primary argument the claim that the only prudent conclusion to be made about British policy is that the policy was, and would continue to be, dangerous to American liberty. At a convention of Virginia's colonial leaders in March of 1775 Patrick Henry offered a resolution to the effect that the colony ought to prepare itself immediately for its defense against British forces. In support of this resolution, Henry reportedly gave the famous speech that concluded with the line "give me liberty, or give me death!" What is interesting here, however, is the argument Henry presents to conclude that fighting is the only reasonable, remaining alternative to the loss of liberty.

Henry begins with the observation that "it is natural to man to indulge in the illusions of hope," that is, in this case, the hope for peaceful reconciliation with a Britain that will protect the colonists' rights. But immediately he asks whether to act from such a hope is "the part of wise men engaged in a great and arduous struggle for

23. *TJ*, I, 125.

liberty." In order to answer that question, he has recourse to the history of the previous ten years. He asks "what there had been in the conduct of the British ministry for the last ten years, to justify those hopes with which gentlemen had been pleased to solace themselves." Noting the British military buildup in the colonies, Henry asks:

> And what have we to oppose them? Shall we try argument? Sir, we have been trying that for the last ten years. Have we anything new to offer on the subject? Nothing. We have held the subject up in every light of which it is capable; but it has been all in vain. Shall we resort to entreaty and humble supplication? What terms shall we find, which have not already been exhausted? Let us not, I beseech you, sir, deceive ourselves longer. Sir, we have done everything that could be done, to avert the storm which is now coming on. We have petitioned—we have remonstrated—we have supplicated—we have prostrated ourselves before the throne, and have implored its interposition to arrest the tyrannical hands of the ministry and parliament. Our petitions have been slighted; our remonstrances have produced additional violence and insult; our supplications have been disregarded; and we have been spurned, with contempt, from the foot of the throne. In vain, after these things, may we indulge in the fond hope of peace and reconciliation.

Thus Henry argues that prudent men must look to the political reality and draw the conclusions that are most likely to be safe to their liberty. It would be foolish, he tells his fellow citizens, to look at the politics of the previous ten years and hope that American liberty is safe from British invasion. There is nothing in that political record to suggest any genuine concern on the part of the British for colonial liberty.

Having made the point that the only conclusion a prudent man can draw from the politics of the preceding ten years is that American liberty is in serious danger under British rule, Henry goes on to argue the importance of acting against budding tyranny as soon as possible. In response to the argument that the Americans are too weak to contest the British militarily, Henry says: "But when shall we be stronger? Will it be the next week, or the next year? Will it be when we are totally disarmed, and when a British guard shall be stationed in every house? Shall we gather strength by irresolution and inaction? Shall we acquire the means of effectual resistance by lying supinely on our backs, and hugging the delusive phantom of Hope, until our enemies shall have bound us hand and foot?"[24] Thus Henry makes

---

24. William Wirt Henry, *Patrick Henry* (3 vols.; New York, 1891), I, 262–65.

the point that tyranny must be combatted in its early stages. Once prudent men appreciate the existence of a design of tyranny—an appreciation they can gain only from a wise estimation of the meaning of events—prudence indicates the need for swift action to forestall the consolidation of the tyranny. Henry's stirring exhortation to fight for liberty is not the product of an ideology that has led him to see conspiracy everywhere. It is the result of a prudent understanding of political reality.

Another American leader during the revolutionary period who understood the prudence of assuming that there was a design to remove American liberty was John Dickinson. In May of 1774 he wrote this statement: "The subject of the present dispute between Great Britain and us, is so generally understood, that to enlarge upon it is needless. We know the *extent* of her claims. We begin to feel the *enforcement* of those claims. We may foresee the consequences of them; for, reason teaching us to infer actions from principles, and events from examples, should convince us, what a perfection of servitude is to be fixed upon us, and our posterity."[25] The passage indicates the prudential nature of the American actions throughout the period preceding the Revolution. Prudence teaches one to infer actions from principles. The principle from which the actions were inferred by the colonists was the principle stated in the Declaratory Act that was behind all the controversial legislation of the period: Parliament had the authority to do whatever it wished to the colonists without regard for their liberty. Because they understood the implications of this principle, the colonial leaders had argued the importance of resisting the various pieces of legislation from the Stamp Act through the Coercive Acts. Rational men also infer events from examples. The examples of the ten years before Dickinson wrote had indicated a persistent willingness on the part of the British to violate the colonists' liberties. Given those examples and their frequency, prudent men could infer only that such attempts would continue in the future and that if allowed to continue, those attempts would end in the destruction of American liberty. This is not ideology. It is the rational calculation of a prudent statesman.

The rhetoric of conspiracy was effect, not cause. The Americans spoke of the existence of a design to remove their liberties not because they had been conditioned to see conspiracies everywhere but because they saw act after act of the British government violate their

25. *JD*, 469.

liberties and they knew that steps must be taken to prevent such acts in the future. There was no ideology that had the Americans in its clutches and caused them to perceive dangers that were not really there.[26] Instead, the Americans reached the rational conclusion that there were real and severe dangers to their liberty posed by the British government, and they used the rhetoric of conspiracy to communicate this danger to the American citizens.[27]

The leaders of the Americans argued for and participated in resistance and finally revolution because they understood three things. First, they knew of the importance of liberty for human beings. Second, they understood that actions undertaken by the British government abridged American liberties and threatened to impose upon America an absolute and arbitrary government. Finally, they understood that despotism must be attacked in its design stage because it is difficult to defeat once it has become well established. Well-informed and well-educated reason led them to act as they did.

The prudence of the Americans in their pursuit of liberty is demonstrated not only by their understanding of the necessity for them to act to maintain their freedom but also by the way in which they acted. They were reluctant to transform their fear for their liberty into revolution partly out of a conviction that British rule had secured liberty effectively and ought to be expected to continue to do so. Another factor contributing to that reluctance was the colonial leaders' understanding of the dangers involved in using violence to address political problems.

That the American concern for liberty was a concern for ordered liberty is clearly shown by the writings of John Adams and John Dickinson. Both understood and stated clearly the need for stability in government if rights were to be secure. Along with their colleagues, they called for peaceful and lawful efforts to redress colonial grievances. Until it became clear that such measures would not work, they called for petitions and nonimportation, and they worried

26. "Does the reaction of the colonists remain inexplicable, or very nearly so, in the absence of the outlook which was, as Bailyn insists, determinative of the political understanding of eighteenth-century Americans? It would not seem so. . . . The imperial-colonial conflict arose from a desire of provincial elites to be free from external control, and from the unwillingness of metropolitan officials to acquiesce in the full development of this condition. Neither the colonial desire to be free, nor the metropolitan desire to assert control, were passions that needed special instruction from the exigencies of eighteenth-century political discourse." Tucker and Hendrickson, *First British Empire*, 208–209.

27. See Harvey C. Mansfield, Jr., *The Spirit of Liberalism* (Cambridge, 1978), 80.

about the dangers of using violence when it was not clearly necessary to preserve liberty. Even Samuel Adams, called by Hutchinson "the grand incendiary," shared this prudent concern for stability in government. In a 1773 letter he wrote that "I have long feared that this unhappy Contest between Britain & America will end in Rivers of Blood. Should this be the Case, America I think may wash her hands in innocence; yet it is the highest prudence to prevent if possible so dreadful a Calamity."[28]

That the American revolutionaries shared this "highest prudence," that they were well schooled in political reality, is demonstrated by their actions in creating governments to replace the British government quickly when the Declaration of Independence was adopted. In many cases the new governments that were needed to ensure order and stability were formed before independence was declared. John Adams, for example, argued for the creation of governments characterized by separation of powers and a balance of the forces within society that would maintain order through the same principles that were used to maintain order under the British constitution.

Bernard Bailyn presents Adams' advocacy of a balanced constitution as evidence of Adams' being ruled by an ideological paranoia, especially with regard to his opinion of Thomas Hutchinson: "He [Hutchinson] wished for stability and peace on the only terms he could conceive of their being firmly established. In his understanding of government he was of course conservative, but no more so than John Adams, who despised him and feared him and attacked him publicly and privately on every possible occasion but whose constitution for the Commonwealth of Massachusetts . . . exhibited to perfection the ideal of balance achieved through the independence and separation of powers which, in an older context, Hutchinson had struggled to retain."[29] Thus Bailyn presents John Adams' political conservatism as evidence of his irrationality: he should have acted with Hutchinson instead of against him because they shared the same concern for stability and peace. But although Bailyn notices an important and instructive fact about Adams, he draws the wrong conclusion from that fact. Indeed Adams was conservative. He was concerned with peace and stability, as were his fellow revolutionaries. The difference between Adams and Hutchinson was not in understanding that human beings need stable government, but in the

28. *SA*, II, 398.
29. Bailyn, *Ordeal*, 377.

fact that Adams and his colleagues understood as well that government ought to secure liberty. There was a fundamental difference between the government Hutchinson argued for and the government Adams argued for. In missing that difference, Bailyn misses what the American Revolution was all about. The difference is that under Adams' government the people ruled themselves whereas under the government Hutchinson argued for, they did not. The difference is that under Adams' government, the people's liberty—their opportunity to make the choices that would determine their own lives, their opportunity to realize the dignity of human beings—was secure. The leaders of the American Revolution argued, worked, and reluctantly fought for peace, stability, and, most important, for liberty. The study of their revolution is the study of the rational pursuit of human liberty.

Index

Adams, Abigail, 90
Adams, John: meaning of the Revolution to, 6; importance of, 14–15, 78–79; "Novanglus" letters, 14, 15, 79–80, 84–86, 88, 90, 121, 164; view of Otis, 16, 17, 25, 27; view of Virginia Resolves, 31, 38–39; view on authority of Parliament, 55, 84–86, 88, 121; view of Catholic church, 72, 81, 112; idea of conspiracy against American colonies, 79–81, 88, 164; "Dissertation on the Canon and Feudal Law," 81–82, 91; view of liberty, 81–83, 90–91, 117, 118, 119, 173, 174–75; view of king's responsibility to colonists, 84–86; view of representation, 84; view of taxation, 84, 123; view of colonial charters, 85; "Instructions of the Town of Boston to Their Representatives," 86–87; on admiralty courts, 86–87; view of salaries of governor and judges, 87–88; conservatism of, 90, 174; view of revolution, 91; view of virtue, 130–50; *Thoughts on Government*, 131–32, 138; view of happiness, 131, 138–41, 149, 150; *A Defence of the Constitutions of Government of the United States*, 132–50; advocacy of balanced constitution, 132–38, 146–50, 174; on executive branch, 133–34, 146; on legislative branch, 134–38, 146; view

of property, 134–35, 139–43; view of Sparta, 143–44; on filling government positions in colonies, 147; view of Hutchinson, 155, 174; view of independence, 155; view of Mayhew's sermon, 156; view of tyranny, 166–67
Adams, Samuel: as propagandist, 3, 61–62; importance of, 14–15; and natural rights doctrine, 62–64, 71–73, 75; on rights of colonists, 62–63, 71–74; view of property, 63–64, 66–67, 74; view of taxation, 63–66, 113, 123; view of representation, 64, 66; view of colonial charters, 65–66, 72–73; view of liberty, 66–67, 68–69, 113, 117; and British influence on colonial government, 67–70, 71; view of British military, 70–71; view of revolution, 73–74, 77, 155, 174; view of authority of Parliament, 74, 114–15, 121; view of Sparta, 75, 143; view of virtue, 75–76, 130, 131; on colonists as British citizens, 162, 163; idea of conspiracy against American colonies, 164; on payment of salaries of governors and judges, 167; view of tyranny, 167, 168
Admiralty courts, 86–87, 102, 115
American colonists: as British citizens, 25, 27, 28, 32–33, 46, 62, 65, 72–73, 121, 162–63; conspiracy against, 59n, 79–81, 88, 164, 168–169, 170, 172–73; Samuel Adams' view of, 62–63,

71–74; king's responsibility toward, 65, 84–86, 93; change in British treatment of, 168–170. See also names of specific leaders

American Revolution: Progressives' view of, 1–6, 9; ideological origins of, 6–8, 12–13; psychological interpretation of, 9–10; revolutionary syndrome and, 9–10; leaders of, 14–15; goal of, 150–52. See also Revolution; names of specific leaders

Andrews, Charles McLean, 1–2

Aristotle, 99, 138, 141, 144–45, 150–51

Army. See British troops

Bailyn, Bernard, 5–11, 153–55, 173n, 174–75

Bancroft, George, 1

Beard, Charles, 2

Becker, Carl, 2–4

Beer, George Louis, 1–2

Bernard, Francis, 31, 79

Boston Massacre, 70

Boston Tea Party, 89–90, 95–96

Brattle, William, 87

British constitution: Otis' views of, 22–23, 25–27, 28; natural rights and, 64; and liberty, 83, 119–24, 162–63; ministers' views of, 160–61

British government: mistakes of, 52–53. See also British constitution; King; Parliament

British troops, 67, 70–71, 88, 96, 102, 115, 165, 170, 171

Brown, B. Katherine, 5

Brown, Robert E., 5

Burke, Edmund, 111–12, 114, 165–66

Catholic church, 72, 81, 112

Charles I, 59, 59n, 156, 158–59

Charters, colonial: Otis' views on, 25, 28; Virginia Resolves and, 33; Dickinson's views on, 46; Samuel Adams' views on, 62–63, 65–66, 72–73; John Adams' views on, 85; significance of, 111

Cicero, 99

Coercive Acts, 67, 95, 102, 115, 165, 172

Colonial government: influence of Townshend Acts on, 49–50; and suspension of New York legislature, 67, 95, 96, 102, 115, 165, 169; and salaries of governors and judges, 68–70, 71, 87–88, 102, 115–16, 165, 167, 170; admiralty courts and, 86–87, 102, 115; jury trials and, 102; filling government positions in, 147

Colonial government salaries, 68–70, 71, 87–88, 102, 115–16, 165, 167, 170

Colonies. See American colonists

Continental Congress, 14, 41, 60, 78, 92, 98, 106, 152, 163

Contract theory, 18–20

Courts. See Admiralty courts

Davidson, Philip, 3

Declaration of Independence, 10–15, 92, 98–109, 152, 155, 163, 165, 166, 174

Declaratory Act, 43, 95, 102, 114, 120, 122, 165, 169, 172

Dickinson, John: Farmer's Letters, 14, 15, 43–60, 128–29, 148, 167, 168; importance of, 14–15; conservatism of, 41, 42, 60; view of independence, 41, 42, 56–59, 155; radicalism of, 42, 51, 56, 60; view of Townshend Acts, 42–60; view of property, 43, 113; view of happiness, 44–45, 46, 51–52, 56, 57–58; view of liberty, 44–47, 51, 53, 56, 58–60, 110, 113, 117–18, 119, 173; view of natural rights doctrine, 46–47; view of taxation, 46, 47, 48, 54–55, 66, 123; on influence of British government on colonial government, 49–50; and right to evaluate government, 51–53; view of authority of Parliament, 55–56, 115, 121; idea of conspiracy against American colonies, 59n, 172; view of virtue, 128–30, 131, 148, 149, 152; view of tyranny, 166–68

Economic determinism, 2–3

England. See British constitution; British government; British troops

Essex Result, 126–28

Federalist, The, 76
Franklin, Benjamin, 41, 80
Freedom. *See* Liberty

Gage, Thomas, 31
George III, 13, 99, 101–103
Gerry, Elbridge, 75
Government. *See* British constitution;
 Colonial government; King;
 Parliament
Governors. *See* Colonial government
 salaries; names of specific governors
Grenville, George, 17, 31

Hancock, John, 3
Happiness: Dickinson's views on, 44–
 45, 46, 51–52, 56–60; Jefferson's
 views on, 99, 101, 103, 118; John
 Adams' views on, 131, 138–41, 149,
 150
Henry, Patrick: importance of, 14–15;
 Virginia Resolves, 14, 15, 30–40; on
 colonists as British citizens, 32–33,
 162–63; view of representation, 33–
 37; view of taxation, 33–37, 39–40,
 123; view of authority of Parliament,
 34–38, 155; and Stamp Act, 38–40;
 on defending against British, 170–72;
 view of tyranny, 171–72
Hooker, Richard, 73
Hutchinson, Thomas, 8, 11, 69, 79–81,
 86, 147, 153–55, 174–75

Independence. *See* American Revolution; Revolution

James II, 22, 23, 29
Jefferson, Thomas: Becker's view of, 4;
 letter of, from John Adams, 6; on need
 for prudent approach, 10–11; and
 Declaration of Independence, 14, 15,
 92, 98–109; importance of, 14–15;
 *Summary View of the Rights of Brit-
 ish America,* 15, 92–98, 100, 102, 103,
 105, 106, 116–17, 123, 164–65, 170;
 Virginia Resolves and, 31, 36, 39; natural rights doctrine and, 92–93, 99–
 101, 103–104, 107–109, 107n, 117–

18; view of authority of Parliament,
 93–97, 102–103, 121; view of representation, 95; view of taxation, 96,
 103–104, 123; complaints against
 king, 97–98, 101–103, 106; view of
 happiness, 99, 101, 103, 118; view of
 liberty, 99, 101, 106–109, 116–17;
 writing of Virginia constitution, 102;
 view of property, 103–104; view of rationality, 104–106, 108; view of duty
 and honor, 108–109; view of revolution, 108; view of colonies' relationship with king, 123–24; view of
 independence, 155; on colonists as
 British citizens, 162; idea of conspiracy against American colonies,
 164–65, 170
Judges. *See* Colonial government
 salaries
Jury trials, 115

King: authority of, 65; Samuel Adams'
 blame of, 74; John Adams' view of authority of, 84–86; colonists' relationship with, 84–86, 93, 123–24;
 Jefferson's complaints against, 97–98,
 101–103, 106; and Declaration of Independence, 101–103

Lee, Arthur, 69, 164
Liberty: taxation and, 26–27; Dickinson's views on, 44–47, 51, 53, 56, 110,
 113, 117–19, 173; and happiness, 44–
 45, 46; and rational behavior, 45–46,
 82, 104–106, 108, 116–18; Montesquieu's definition of, 53n, 114; Samuel Adams' views on, 66–67, 68–69,
 112, 117; virtue and, 75–76, 151–52;
 John Adams' views on, 81–83, 90–91,
 117–19, 173–75; ordered, 90, 173;
 Jefferson's views on, 99, 101, 106–
 109, 116–17; American tradition of,
 111–12, 155–56, 165–66; Otis' views
 on, 111, 117, 119; and right to property, 113–14; British contributions to,
 119; constitutional arguments for,
 119–24; importance of, 125; ministers' views on, 156–61; prudence and,

165, 167–68, 170–75; defense of, 170–72

Lincoln, Charles H., 2

Locke, John, 19, 21, 23, 24, 63, 73–75, 90, 99, 113, 159, 160

Machiavelli, Niccolo, 110–11, 140
Maier, Pauline, 62, 78
Main, Jackson Turner, 5
Mayhew, Jonathan, 156–61
Military. See British troops
Miller, John C., 62
Monarchy. See King
Montesquieu, Charles-Louis de Secondat, 53n, 66, 68, 73, 114, 141
Morgan, Edmund S., 4–5, 147
Morgan, Helen M., 4–5
Mutiny Act, 67

Natural rights doctrine: in the Declaration of Independence, 12–13; Otis' views on, 21–24; Dickinson's views on, 46–47; Samuel Adams' views on, 62–64, 71–73, 75; Jefferson's views on, 92–93, 99–101, 103–104, 107–109, 107n, 117–18; ministers' views on, 159–60; shift toward argument of, 163–64
Nedham, Marchmont, 134
New York legislature, 67, 95, 96, 102, 115, 165, 169

Oliver, Andrew, 80, 154
Oliver, Peter, 80
Otis, James: importance of, 14–15; The Rights of the British Colonies Asserted and Proved, 15, 17–29; John Adams' view of, 16, 25, 27; writs of assistance and, 16–17; opposition to the Sugar Act, 18–29; on origin of government, 18–20; view of property, 20–21; and natural rights doctrine, 21–24; A Vindication of the British Colonies, 28, 28n; view of revolution, 29; reaction to Stamp Act, 31; view of liberty, 111, 117, 119; view of taxation, 113; view of authority of Parliament, 121, 122–23; on colonists as British citizens, 162

Paine, Thomas, 43, 126
Parliament: colonists' views on, 4–5; Otis' views on, 25–29, 121, 122–23; Henry's views on, 35–38, 155; trade regulation and, 36, 48, 54–55, 85, 94, 121–22; Dickinson's views on, 55–56, 115, 121; John Adams' views on, 55, 84–86, 121; Samuel Adams' views on, 64–65, 74, 114–15, 121; suspension of New York legislature, 67, 95, 96, 102, 115, 165, 169; authority of, 79, 80, 88, 114–15, 120–22, 169, 172; Jefferson's views on, 93–97, 102–103, 121; and Declaration of Independence, 102; and American liberty, 111–12, 165–66. See also Representation; Taxation; names of specific acts
Patriotism, 148–49
Pitt, William, 111
Private property. See Property
Progressives, 1–4, 5, 6, 163
Property: Otis' views on, 20–21; taxation and, 26; Dickinson's views on, 44, 113; Samuel Adams' views on, 63–64, 66–67, 74; Jefferson's views on, 103–104; and liberty, 113–14; John Adams' views on, 134–35, 139–43
Pythagoras, 140

Quartering Act, 102, 165, 169

Randolph, John, 106
Randolph, Peyton, 36
Religious toleration, 72
Representation: Otis' views on, 22, 26–29; Virginia Resolves and, 34–37; Samuel Adams' views on, 64, 66; John Adams' views on, 84; Jefferson's views on, 95; importance of, 123
Revenue acts. See Taxation
Revolution: Otis' views on, 23, 29; Dickinson's views on, 56–60; and right to happiness, 57–58; Samuel Adams' views on, 73–74, 77, 174; John Adams' views on, 91; Jefferson's views on, 100, 108; dangers of, 104; and protection of individual rights, 128; prudence and, 162, 165, 167–68,

170–75; in Declaration of Independence, 165, 166; Henry's views on, 170–72. *See* American Revolution
Rights. *See* Happiness; Liberty; Natural rights doctrine; Property

Schlesinger, Arthur Meier, 2–3
Search warrants. *See* Writs of assistance
Slavery, 24, 112, 113, 115–16, 117, 165, 166, 170
Socrates, 140
Soldiers. *See* British troops
Sparta, 75, 143–44
Stamp Act: Hutchinson's views on, 8; Virginia Resolves and, 15, 30–40; colonial reaction to, 16, 30–31, 39, 103, 113, 114, 120, 172; purpose of, 30; protest against, 31, 154; repeal of, 43, 63, 120, 129; compared with the Townshend Acts, 44, 47–48; Dickinson's views on, 46; Samuel Adams' views on, 63, 73; violations of, 66; John Adams' views on, 79, 84; admiralty courts and, 87; Jefferson's opposition to, 95; importance of, 155, 165; Henry's reaction to, 163
Stamp Act Congress, 47
Sugar Act, 17–18, 30, 95, 155

Tacitus, 88
Taxation: internal versus external, 26, 28, 47–48; Otis' views on, 26–29, 113; Virginia Resolves and, 33–37, 39–40, 113; trade duties versus, 36, 48, 54–55, 85; colonial resistance to, 38–40; Dickinson's views on, 46, 47, 66, 123; Samuel Adams' views on, 63–66, 113, 123; John Adams' views on, 84, 123; Jefferson's views on, 96, 103–104, 123; Henry's views on, 123

Tea Act, 67, 71, 84, 89, 103, 113, 114, 165
Tocqueville, Alexis de, 142, 148–49
Townshend Acts: Dickinson's views on, 42–60, 128–30, 149, 167; Samuel Adams' views on, 63, 66; repeal of, 67, 71, 89; colonial views on, 84, 95, 103, 113, 114, 165, 169; resistance to, 167
Trevelyan, Sir George Otto, 1
Turgot, Anne Robert Jacques, 132–33
Tyranny: Henry's views on, 37, 38, 170–72; Dickinson's views on, 53, 166–68; Samuel Adams' views on, 68, 167; John Adams' views on, 81–82, 88–89, 145, 146, 166, 167; Jefferson's views on, 95–96, 106, 170; of Parliament, 114; Mayhew's views on, 158, importance of combatting, 165–68, 170–72

Vattel, Emmerich de, 19, 73
Virginia Resolves, 14, 15, 30–40, 43, 113, 116, 155, 163, 168
Virtue: liberty and, 75–76, 128–30, 151–52; Samuel Adams' views on, 75–76, 130, 131; importance of, 125–26; Dickinson's views on, 128–30, 131, 148, 149, 152; as public-spiritedness, 128–30; John Adams' views on, 130–50; traditional moral values, 130–31, 143; difficulties in attaining, 140–42; Montesquieu's concept of, 141; and wealth, 141–43; rationality and, 151

Warren, James, 75
Whig historians, 1
Whigs, radical, 6–7, 8
Wise, John, 159
Wood, Gordon, 9–15, 78, 125, 126–28, 132
Writs of assistance, 16–17, 86, 88, 155